THE
VICTORIAN
CELEBRATION
OF DEATH

James Stevens Curl

THE VICTORIAN CELEBRATION OF DEATH

The architecture and planning of the 19th century necropolis with some observations on the ephemera of the Victorian funeral and a special chapter on cemeteries and funeral customs in America.

The Partridge Press
Detroit

First published in the United States in
1972 by the Partridge Press, Gale
Research Company, Book Tower,
Detroit, Mich 48226.
Library of Congress Catalog Card No
70-184048.

Printed in Great Britain.

for

Eileen

who could never enthuse about cemeteries

but who understood

Contents

Illustrations

[ix]

Illustrations at the chapter openings

*Illustrations not otherwise acknowledged are from the collection of
the author, or are photographs and drawings by him.*

Preface

*The cemetery is an open space among the ruins, covered in winter
with violets and daisies. It might make one in love with death,
to think that one should be buried in so sweet a place.*
From the Preface to Adonais: *Percy Bysshe Shelley
(1792-1822)*

THE PURPOSE OF THIS BOOK is to express lucidly and, it is hoped, entertainingly, the reasons for the Victorian Celebration of Death, and to provide a history of that celebration together with its physical manifestations.

We are all familiar with the presence in our towns and cities of those huge burial grounds and cemeteries laid out in the nineteenth century. Both Europe and America possess examples in abundance, but few people know or appreciate them. To most persons a cemetery is a place to be avoided.

The grand cemeteries of the last century were showpieces at the time of their creation. They were products of a radical reform movement just as significant in the history of western civilisation as those other political and sanitary reforms which were a feature of the liberal climate of the epoch. As a result of the ignorance of the importance of the nineteenth-century cemeteries, they are in danger of being destroyed, since appreciation of their merits is non-existent or exists only in a minority of students of the period. Many cemeteries have been destroyed; it is feared that many, many more will be consigned to oblivion before a few will finally be preserved in part. It is tragic that in an age when so much lip service is paid to conservation the cemeteries are not appreciated as they should be.

Great surprise is often expressed when an interest in cemeteries and other aspects of a Celebration of Death is declared. Such an interest is today regarded almost as a perversion: graveyards, cemeteries, and the paraphernalia of death are in the same position in the conversations of polite society as was sex some years ago. The aversion of eyes from the hearse; the studied avoidance of a glance at a passing coffin; the hurried disposal of corpses in the municipal incinerator with next to no ceremony; and the somewhat glazed and embarrassed expressions on the faces

A Victorian funeral. 'Six black horses with plumes of black ostrich feathers pulled this gorgeous object.' Note the feather-pages, outriders, mutes, wands, and batons. Note also the immense canopy of ostrich feathers atop the hearse, and note especially the poor district!

of many who pass by a cemetery, a burial ground, or an undertaker's shop are witness to an extraordinary change in public taste in the last few decades. Fashion has played its part, of course. The post-war generation, and indeed the post-first war generation rejected the dark romantic gloom of Victoriana, and demanded an unmysterious church, a neatly clipped garden of rest, a bright and shining world. The leafy melancholy of the Victorian cemetery; the dark mourning of Victorian clothes; and the sombre hush of the Victorian parlour were no longer acceptable. Indeed, the contemporary trend is to look on the Victorian Celebration of Death as something of a joke. In a way, this view is an over-compensation for the current fashion to make as little fuss about death as possible. Yet there is something about the Victorian Celebration of Death that is touching, pathetic, and rather absurd: it would be a great mistake if we were to dismiss it as hypocrisy, commercialism, or fraud. We are much less realistic about death today, for our society is engaged in a conspiracy to pretend that death does not exist, corpses, bones, funerals, and mourning being kept well out of sight and segregated from everyday life.

The pro-cremation propaganda has been enormously successful since the war, although the arguments put forward that cremation is somehow more economical, 'saves land', and so forth are demonstrably false. The huge cemeteries laid out in the nineteenth century provide badly needed open spaces in populous areas, and they contain fine planting which has now matured, so that their benefits as amenity spaces are incalculable. The churchyards of the City of London are now oases of quietude amid the bustle of daily life, and are prized by persons who desire nothing more than somewhere beautiful and peaceful in which to rest awhile. With the decline in religious observance there is clearly a question mark hanging over the churches themselves. It is my contention that the churches and cemeteries will become sanctuaries of sanity and peace within the turmoil of city life, and so it is imperative to preserve them for what will be a truly religious function. The graveyards themselves are already providing temporary havens for the living, where once they gave temporary accommodation to the dead.

The ephemeral objects of the Celebration of Death are not only the cemeteries, tombstones, and monuments, which, in any case, were never intended to be impermanent. They are the expressions of social position and status found in coffin plates and handles, in hearses, in mourning-cards, and in dress. They are the faded mementos of another age: the black-edged mourning-envelope; the electrotyped flowers and leaves of wreaths under glass domes; the embossed patterns of the borders around verses celebrating death.

The fascinating story of the agitation, of the reforms, of the scandals and of the abuses which are part of the history must be told, and a study of the architecture, planting, and planning of the great Victorian cemeteries has been long overdue. The eminent architects and others who created the stately buildings of the nineteenth-century necropolis and its Arcadian landscapes were often famous for other works, but the design of cemeteries has been curiously neglected by architectural historians. It is this general neglect together with the pressing need to provide a history of the best of the early cemeteries before they are destroyed that has prompted me to write this book.

I acknowledge my debt to many sources, including *Old and New London*, by Thornbury and Walford; Charles Knight's *London*, revised by Walford; Puckle's *Funeral Customs*; and many other volumes which are listed in full in the Bibliography. I am especially grateful to Mr Malyon and the General Cemetery Company for permitting me to inspect the minutes of the company and for allowing me access to the catacombs and to the chapels; to Mrs G. Walker for help with regard to the East London Cemetery at Plaistow; to Mr Stanley of the Great Northern Cemetery; and to superintendents of cemeteries and crematoria too numerous to list. I thank them all for their courtesy and help, especially with records and answers to my almost interminable questions. I am grateful to the Editor of *The Journal of the Royal Institute of British Architects* for permission to reproduce material of mine previously published. I should also like to thank Mr David Dean and the staff of the RIBA library for their help. The staff of the RIBA Drawings Collection have also been of great assistance to me. The staffs of the Bodleian Library, Oxford; of the British Museum Reading Room; of the Public

Record Office; and of the various public libraries I have consulted also have my gratitude. I especially thank the staff of the Kensington and Chelsea and Camden Public Libraries.

John Gerrard has been very kind, and made valuable suggestions in the research period. Peter B. Bond very helpfully granted me permission to quote from his published work, for which I am very grateful.

I thank all those friends who have perambulated the strange world of the Victorian Necropolis with me, and I owe an especial debt to my wife, who not only ventured into the explorations of the silent oceans of tombstones with me, but also read my manuscripts and offered invaluable criticism and advice. A. H. Buck very kindly read the typescripts and corrected many of my worst excesses.

Again I thank my old friend Rodney Roach who helped with the processing of the pictures. My handwriting was translated into typescript by Eleonore Wetzler and Kathleen Hill, who have my sincere sympathy as well as my gratitude.

If I have omitted to mention any other helper, it has been unintentional, for I thank all those who aided me with the project.

James Stevens Curl
Oxford and London, 1970-1

1 The Victorian Funeral

All things that we ordained festival,
Turn from their office to black funeral;
Our instruments to melancholy bells,
Our wedding cheer to sad burial feast,
Our solemn hymns to sullen dirges change,
Our bridal flowers serve for a buried corse,
And all things change them to the contrary.
                    William Shakespeare: Romeo and Juliet

Mr Jukes' truck-hearse

The Victorian Funeral Procession

A Victorian funeral procession was an extraordinary sight. The leading coach was the hearse, and often it was preceded by mutes and other attendants carrying the trappings of mourning. The hearse itself was black, with glass sides, sometimes etched with designs resembling those in the glass of the public houses. There was much silver and gold decoration, and under what was a huge canopy of black ostrich feathers atop the hearse lay the coffin, shiny and polished, with bolection mouldings, expensive metal handles and engraved inscribed plates. Sometimes the coffin was covered with black, purple, or very dark green cloth, fixed to the wood by brass, silver, or gilt-headed nails. The sides of the coffin were visible through the glass panels, and the interior of the hearse was ablaze with flowers. Six black horses with plumes of black ostrich feathers pulled this gorgeous object, sometimes at walking pace, if feather-pages, outriders, mutes, wands, and batons were to compose the full 'extras' of the funeral (preface). There were attempts to cut costs by dispensing with horses, but these were unsuccessful because of the distances involved in travelling to the new cemeteries. Mr H. W. Jukes invented a 'carriage for walking funerals' which had a cross-handle in front for two persons to haul by, and two handles behind for assisting to push the 'Truck-Hearse' up hills or to retard it when going down a hill (page 2).

Behind the hearse came the coaches, each containing mourners in the strict order prescribed by etiquette. The gentlemen wore full mourning, with crape bands round their top hats, while the ladies were dressed in black, with black veils, many yards of crape, black-edged handkerchiefs held to eyes, and black gloves. The deaf ladies carried special 'mourning' ear trumpets of 'Vulcanite' covered with black silk, and decorated with lace and ribbon, on silk cords. Mourning-fans of black ostrich feathers on tortoiseshell sticks were also carried, and mourning-jewellery of jet, cameo, pearl, gold, or silver would be worn. The coaches in which mourners travelled usually had the blinds drawn. Richer families had special family monograms made for the mourning-coaches and for the decoration of the horses' harness (below).

The mourning-coach shown there is one of the many in the Duke of Wellington's funeral procession which took place on 18 November 1852. This was possibly the grandest

An early Victorian mourning-coach. Note the crape round the top hats, the rich hangings on the saddles and coach, and the black plumes carried by the attendants (from Alken and Sala's Folding Panoramic View of the Duke of Wellington's Funeral which took place on 18 November 1852)

of all Victorian funerals, the hearse being preceded by large contingents from the forces, and the funeral car itself being without doubt the most magnificent of the century. Today this car may be seen in the crypt of St Paul's Cathedral. It was made of metal from guns captured at the battle of Waterloo, and was designed by Superintendent Redgrave and Professor Gottfried Semper, the details relating to woven fabrics and heraldry being designed by Professor Octavius Hudson. The substantial six-wheeled waggon had a large superstructure decorated with banners and weapons, and on the magnificent velvet pall lay the crimson-covered coffin with the Duke's cheese-cutter hat resting on it. Over the whole structure was a canopy complete with ostrich feathers and rich hangings. Twelve horses were needed to pull this triumphal car, all of which wore black ostrich plumes on their heads, while velvet saddle-cloths emblazoned with heraldry covered their flanks.

Nelson's funeral car was also magnificent, though naturally much lighter and more elegant, and was designed on the lines of the *Victory* complete with figurehead; the whole being covered by a draped canopy topped by six plumes of black ostrich feathers (page 5).

Wellington's funeral was the apotheosis of all Victorian funerals, grander than that of either the prince consort or the Queen. Prince Albert himself devised the duke's obsequies, and saw to it that crape was everywhere used with a prodigality suitable for the Celebration of Death of the 'Last Great Englishman'. Even the crowds who turned out to see the procession were dressed in the deepest mourning, and every vantage point was taken to see the huge procession pass. The soldiers carried their arms reversed, muffled drums beat time to the 'Dead March', and the heavy funeral car rumbled along, preceded by black horses and large numbers of soldiers, and followed by many

Lord Nelson's funeral car. The funeral took place on 9 January 1806

coaches carrying the chief mourners. Winston Churchill's funeral more than a century later was a poor show in comparison.

The duke and other illustrious Victorians were given the full treatment, and such grandeur deserves mention here, but it is with the more everyday funeral that I am most concerned. Let us therefore return to the funeral procession with which the chapter began. Steadily it made its way from the house of the deceased along the main roads leading out of the town, sometimes making a detour to go through important areas so that the maximum display could be achieved. Once out of a salubrious district, however, the mutes and others on foot climbed up to the seats on the carriages, and the procession made its way at a brisk trot. It could never be said that the Victorians buried their dead without ceremony. Apart from the immediate family, all the distant relatives would be present. A great family reunion was brought about by the death of one of its members. Friends, business associates, acquaintances would all appear, since cards had gone out to every conceivably interested person. A dozen or sometimes more coaches therefore followed the hearse; the women would not necessarily attend the interment but might be present at the religious ceremony in the church or chapel.

The procession passed out of the more populous parts of the town to a suburban district. It turned in through a huge gateway flanked by lodges, and stopped. The mutes with silk dresses, the assistants 'with silk hatbands and gloves, truncheons and wands'[1] then descended from their seats on the carriages, and the procession once more moved forward at walking pace. It slowly passed by tall trees, among which were obelisks, mausolea, and urns. The avenue led to a building in the centre of the cemetery. Outside this chapel the procession stopped.

In dignified calm the mourners entered the chapel. All stood as the coffin was carried in to rest on the bier or catafalque. The funeral service could end with the coffin slowly descending through the floor to the catacombs beneath on a mechanically operated catafalque, or the ceremony could finish at the place of burial outside in the cemetery. The form of service if Anglican was held in the Anglican chapel in the consecrated ground. Dissenters had their own chapels in the unconsecrated ground, and Roman Catholics and Jews usually had their own cemeteries. The richer dead were carried to their splendid mausolea, which were lying open, and the coffins were reverently placed on their shelves to the accompaniment of the end of the burial service. The cast-iron doors were closed and locked. Many dead, however, were buried in the earth or in brick-lined graves. The poor were interred in common graves, several deep.

[6]

The Victorian Funeral as a Social Necessity

The Victorian undertaking trade encouraged expensive and substantial funerals, so that the quantities of oak, elm, lead, brass, bronze, silk, linen, and other materials committed to the earth in the nineteenth century are appalling to contemplate. I have recently inspected some coffins dating from the 1860s which were exhumed from a London cemetery: the oak was 1¼in thick, and the brass furniture was magnificent.

Ostentatious displays of grief were very much required by Victorian society. The blinds of the house where a death had occurred were drawn, and on the day of the funeral one or two 'mutes' were posted on the front doorstep of the house of mourning. The 'mutes' were paid by the undertaker to assume melancholy expressions, frock coats, and top hats. They carried crape-covered wands, and were not only symbolic of the visitation of death, but of the guards at the bier and of the professional mourners of antiquity. Door knockers and door knobs were extravagantly beribboned with crape. At public funerals of distinguished personages buildings on the processional route were hung with many hundreds of yards of crape, an extension of the 'private' displays on houses. Blinds were drawn on the processional route, and hats were automatically doffed.

The examination of an undertaker's account of 1824 gives some idea of the lengths to which the Celebration of Death was to go in Victorian times. Even in that year of 1824, we read of 'a strong coffin with white sattin lining and pillow, mattress, sheets, strong outside Oak Case covered with superfine black cloth, best silvered Nails and rich ornaments, silvered black Ostrich feathers, man to carry Do.'. Other items included silk scarves, hatbands and gloves, feather-pages and wands, mutes on horseback, silk dressings for poles, best black velvets and sets of ostrich feathers, cloaks, pages, truncheons, crape, attendants, rooms on the road, and coachmen, turnpikes and featherman; bringing the total cost to £803 11s. 0d.! This was a fantastic sum of money for the period, and by the 1870s an expensive middle-class funeral could cost well over a thousand pounds, not including the construction of an elaborate tomb. It is hardly surprising that a poor working-class family could be ruined by attempts to emulate such display.

The 'dismal trade' became a highly lucrative one, and the Victorian undertaker, although never quite 'respectable' in the eyes of society, could afford to live in the best areas and to run a luxurious house. Others grew wealthy on the proceeds of the trappings of mourning, which, especially for women, was deep and prolonged. Whole families, including servants, were expected to wear mourning when a death occurred in the household. 'Mourning-jewellery' became popular, black enamel being a material much in vogue, white being substituted in the case of a young person or a child. Brooches and rings frequently contained miniatures painted on ivory, sometimes representing the deceased person, but more often showing allegories of death, including tombstones, urns, weeping willows and other emblems. Seed pearls were often set in jewellery as symbols of tears and for general enrichment. Lockets were also popular, enclosing photographs, daguerrotypes, or miniatures of the dead person, or sometimes a lock of hair.

Turquoise was regarded as being affected by the ill-health of the wearer, and it was thought to remain dull after death, only regaining its colour when worn by a person in good health. Opals were looked on as symbols of bad luck, and were sometimes worn instead of pearls to denote grief. Jet, however, was by far the most common material for mourning-jewellery, and was often set in silver. Whitby was the centre of the jet industry in Britain.

[8]

Mourning-dress itself is associated with a deeply rooted fear of the dead returning. When veiled and cloaked in black, the living were thought to be invisible to the dead, and this was especially so when the dead were buried at night. Since black symbolises night, and is really an absence of colour, it is best fitted to express mourning. Mourning was obligatory in Victorian times, and if the customs were not complied with, it was reckoned to be a sign of disrespect or worse. Even black wedding-dresses were worn by brides who had been recently bereaved. Pressure was brought by neighbours and by relatives to ensure compliance with the mourning-customs of the period, even in cases of great poverty. Puckle[2] relates the story of a servant girl who married a house painter. The young husband was shortly afterwards killed, and his widow went into modest mourning which aroused the admiration of her former employer. This gentleman was therefore shocked several days later to meet the girl, this time completely swathed in crape. When asked why she had gone to such extravagance, she tearfully replied that her neighbours and relations had made life unbearable for her, suggesting that if she did not wear a widow's bonnet complete with streamers, veil, and crape, it would be a proof that she had been living in sin or at least that she had not been 'properly married'.

Puckle also tells of a death in a respectable street in a London suburb. The family determined to resist the usual ostentation. The undertaker was asked to provide a plain elm coffin without ornaments, but he was horrified, suggesting that only polished oak was suitable for the district.[3]

Poor families appeared in new black dresses almost as soon as a death had taken place. Impossible though it might seem, it was nearly always done. Burial clubs existed to which small amounts were paid weekly, so that money was

[9]

MOURNING DEPARTMENT.

DRESS FABRICS.

BLACK SERGE, SAIL CLOTH, &c.

	Per yard.
Estamene Serge, shrunk, 40 to 43 in.	1/2½, 1/4½, 1/6½, 1/8½
" " 43 to 48 in.	1/11, 2/3, 2/8, 3/0
" " 54 in.	3/3, 3/8, 3/11, 4/3, 4/11
" " Heavy, 54 in.	3/2, 3/11, 4/6, 4/11
Diagonal Cheviot, 45 in.	1/8½, 1/11
Coating Twill, 42 to 46 in.	1/9, 2/3, 2/8
	2/1, 2/4½, 2/7, 2/11
Union, 27 in.	0/9½
Sail Cloth, pirle finish, 46 in.	2/4½, 2/11

BLACK CASHMERE, MERINO, &c.

	Per yard.
Cashmere, French, 47 in.	1/11½, 2/4½, 2/7, 3/2, 3/11
Merino " 42 to 46 in.	
	1/6½, 1/10, 1/11½, 2/5, 2/10, 3/4, 3/11
Cashmere, Indian, (so-called), 46 in.	2/6, 3/3
" Foule, 45 in.	1/8½
Paramatta, 45 in.	4/6, 4/11
Crape Cloth, Venetian, 44 in.	1/9½, 2/1, 2/6, 3/2

BLACK ALPACA, MOHAIR, &c.

	Per yard.
Alpaca, plain, 29 in.	0/8, 0/10½, 1/0½
" 43 to 45 in.	1/6½, 1/11, 2/3
" 48 in.	2/9, 3/0, 3/6, 3/11
" Fancy 44 to 46 in.	2/4½, 3/0
" Sicilian, 54 in.	2/4, 2/11, 3/3, 4/0, 4/11
Fancy Mohair, 44 in.	2/9, 3/0, 3/7

BLACK VOILE, EOLIENNE, &c.

	Per yard.
Voile Wool, plain, 46 in.	1/11½, 2/2, 2/8, 3/0, 3/3
" Plumetis, 44 in.	3/2, 3/9
" de Soie, 46 in.	3/2, 3/9
" Rayé, 45 in.	2/5, 2/7
" Plumetis, 44 in.	3/11
Eolienne, silk and Wool, 44 to 47 in.	2/6, 2/11, 3/3,
	3/11, 4/6
" Ondine " 47 in.	6/6
Crêpe de Chine, silk and wool, 47 in.	3/3, 3/6, 4/3
Crepoline " 45 "	2/4

BLACK CRAPE (Courtauld's).

	Per yard.
Showerproof, 30 in.	3/9, 4/6
" 42 "	5/9, 6/9, 8/6

BLACK FANCY FABRICS.

	Per yard.
Bengaline, Broche, silk and wool, 47 in., new designs	6/6
Majolique " " 42 to 46 " "	4/3 to 4/9
Crepon " " 46 "	4/11
Fancy Wool " 44 " "	from 2/4
Crepoline, Embroidered 46 "	2/11

BLACK GRENADINE, BAREGE, &c.

	Per yard.
Grenadine, plain, 45 in.	2/4, 3/0, 3/11
" fancy, 42 to 46 in.	from 2/0
" canvas, 46 in.	2/2, 2/9, 3/6
" silk, plain, 46 in.	4/11
Tringlette, silk and wool, 45 in.	4/1
Barege, plain, 45 in.	3/1
Guipure, silk and wool, fancy stripes, 46 in.	
	3/11, 4/9, 4/11

BLACK SATIN CLOTH, POPLIN, &c.

	Per yard.
Satin Cloth, 44 in.	2/3, 3/0, 3/3
Poplin Cord, 46"	2/4 to 3/11
Metz " 44 "	2/9, 3/6

BLACK VENETIAN AND AMAZON CLOTH, VIGOGNE, &c.

	Per yard.
Venetian Cloth, 44 in.	1/10½
Amazon " 49 "	2/7½
" " 50 "	3/6, 3/11
" " 54 "	4/9, 5/6, 6/6
Vigogne (so-called) 46 in.	from 2/6

BLACK NUNS' VEILING, &c.

	Per yard.
Nuns' Veiling, 45 in.	2/1
" cloth, 45 in.	1/3½, 1/6
Crêpe, Taffeta, 46 in.	1/8½
San Toy, silk and wool, 44 in.	3/6

BLACK LININGS AND FOUNDATIONS.

	Per yard.
Italian Cloth, 54 in.	1/10½, 2/1, 2/6
Moirette, 24 in.	1/6½
" 40 in.	2/9
" satin stripes, 40 in.	from 2/9
Moreen, 37 in.	1/4, 1/7½, 1/10
Linenette, 44 in.	0/6
" 44 " light make	0/6
Croisélle, 40 in.	0/9
Silkoline, 40 "	0/9½
Sateen, 30 in.	0/7, 0/8½
Taffaline, 40 in.	0/7

For Mantles		see page 743
" Gloves		" 806
" Ribbons		" 808
" Silk Neckerchiefs and Scarfs		" 809

For Fichus, Bows, and Jabots		see page 811
" Widows' Collars and Cuffs		" 815
" Jewellery		" 818
" Handkerchiefs		" 819

SPECIAL ATTENTION GIVEN TO ALL MOURNING ORDERS.

FUNERALS arranged and conducted both in Town and Country at strictly moderate charges. Cremations. Embalming. Portrait Sculpture.

Telegrams: "Auxiliary, London." See Advt., ARMY & NAVY AUXILIARY DEPARTMENTS.

Valuations of Real and Personal Property for Probate and other purposes.

Page from the catalogue of the Army & Navy Stores, London
always available from the club funds to pay for funerals
and mourning-dress. Pawn-shops and cast-off clothes from
the richer sections of society enabled the poor to emulate
as best they could the required custom of the day. 'The

[10]

breathless smell of warm black crape', as Dickens described it, was everywhere prevalent in the house of death. Dresses were heavily trimmed with the material, and even under-clothes were trimmed with black lace. Capes, handkerchiefs, shawls, bonnets, veils, indoor caps, pinafores, boas, and even parasols were adapted for mourning, with black silk, braid, tassels, and the inevitable crape.

The idea of a *Magasin de Deuil*, or establishment exclusively devoted to the sale of mourning-costumes and of the paraphernalia necessary for a nineteenth-century funeral, appears to have originated as an adaptation of the *Mercerie de lutto*. The French mourning-emporium was copied by British stores, and mourning-departments became usual in all the larger shops. Jay's London General Mourning Warehouse, Regent Street, was founded in 1841, and it appears to have been a unique establishment in London. It later expanded to include 'not only all that is necessary for mourning, but also departments devoted to dresses of a more general description, although the colours are confined to such as could be worn for either full or half mourning'. Black silks were a speciality of the house, and continental journals fre-quently announced that '*la maison Jay de Londres a fait de forts achats*'.[4] Indeed, Jay's flourished on the sale of the unchanging materials, such as silks, crapes, paramattas, cashmeres, *grenadines*, and *tulles*. 'The fame of a great house of business . . . rests more upon its integrity and the expedi-tion with which commands are executed than anything else. To secure the very best goods, and to have them made up in the best taste and in the latest fashion, is one of the principal aims of the firm, which is not unmindful of legitimate economy. For this purpose, every season com-petent buyers visit the principal silk marts of Europe, such as Lyons, Genoa, and Milan, for the purpose of purchasing all that is best in quality and pattern. Immediate communication with the leading designers of fashions in Paris has not been neglected; and it may be safely said of this great house of business, that if it is modelled on a mediaeval Italian principle, it has missed no opportunity to assimilate to itself every modern improvement.'[5] Jay's later became a general fashion house, but it is interesting to remember how its fortunes were founded.

The Victorian Funeral nearly always took place from the house of the deceased. It was customary to hold a feast at the house, where the women would dominate the proceedings. This feast in certain districts took place before the funeral, but in others it was held afterwards. At the actual burial it was more usual for men alone to attend, the rigours of both the climate and the experience being reckoned to be too much for the weaker sex. The feast in the houses of the poor was a magnificent affair too, for it was regarded as a point of honour to feed the mourners as well as could possibly be managed, with much ham, cider, and ale. In the north of England ham was a meat especially thought fit for consumption at funerals.

It was often the custom to have the funeral feast provided by the undertaker. The catering would include sherry, ham, pies, port, and cakes. Jelly and trifle were especial funeral treats. The feast stands out as a feature of the obsequies of all times. The viewing of the body might be thought likely to put some people off their food, but the Victorians do not appear to have suffered from such problems. Originally, viewing the body was to satisfy all that the corpse was truly dead and that no foul play had been committed. Obviously the family could then look forward to a legitimate share-out of the wealth of the deceased, and having travelled long distances to be so assured, could then partake of a funeral feast as an act of communion with other members of the group and with the corpse itself. The funeral meal was at one time known as the *averil*, at which crisp bread (or cake) and ale were provided. Thus originated the simnel cake, a 'soul-bread', which was the main symbolic gift of the departed to his surviving relatives. The humble symbolic meal became, in the nineteenth century, a huge feast, where the heavy mahogany groaned under loads of food. Frequently the *averil* was held after the burial, and, especially in Yorkshire, was celebrated in a hostelry.[6] In many districts the wake before the funeral was accompanied by much liquor, a custom partly derived from the ancient symbolic feasts, partly to show how hospitable the families were, and partly for the functional reason of fortifying the mourners against the odour of decay and the often inclement weather at the interment. Feasts in mid-Victorian times became status symbols, and families of all classes vied with their neighbours in terms both of display of funeral magnificence and of the provision of victuals. Curious terminology was used at feasts. For example, a 'mute' might whisper mournfully to one of the assembled company that 'the corpse's brother' wished to take wine with him.[7] This curious way of putting things demonstrates how far the original significance of the feast as a gift from the departed had been preserved in Victorian times. The corpse was still the most important person at the feast, and people were identified by their relationship with it.

Accessories and Monuments

Mourning-cards were another phenomenon of the Victorian Celebration of Death. These were supplied by the undertaker, specially printed for the particular funeral in black and silver on white, and frequently embossed with traditional symbols of grief: the inverted torch, the weeping willow, the shrouded urn, and kneeling female mourners. These cards were in turn mounted on highly ornamental

Victorian mourning-cards with embossed designs. Note how classical these designs are compared with the mourning-card mount shown on page 16. The classical designs are very late for 1876, possibly because of the innate conservatism of East-Enders

[14]

embossed fretted 'memorial-card mounts', usually black and silver with patterns of inverted torches, palms, broken columns, ivy, and much Gothic ornament (Page 16). The whole was then framed and glazed, and kept in the house of bereavement along with *immortelles,* samplers, and other accessories. Black velvet backgrounds were sometimes used as the mounts for mourning-cards, and often the cards were hand-coloured, sometimes incorporating tinted photographs or silhouettes of the deceased.

Naturally, mourning-cards needed mourning-envelopes, and black-edged envelopes and notepaper became obligatory. Black sealing-wax, black stamp boxes, black ink, and mourning-pens were not unusual. Undertakers' trade cards were suitably melancholic in design, and trade catalogues, headed trade paper, including invoice paper, were all carefully produced to appear to be in keeping with the 'dismalness' of the events with which they were concerned.

The cards were intended as reminders of the dead so that the recipient would be sure to offer prayers for the dead and for the bereaved family. The card itself was modest, containing usually the name and age of the dead person and various symbols of grief. Possibly some text or verse might be added, as well as the date and place of burial. The wording was often of the doggerel type:

> A sudden death, a mind contented;
> Living beloved, dead lamented.

or

> Adieu! my sweet one, sleep in peace
> Upon thy pillow lone and chill;
> Thy little life was doomed to cease—
> But ah! I fondly love thee still.

and

> Oh, fond and loving spirit! thou,
> Far, far away from one art now.

Victorian memorial-card mount. It is an embossed specimen, with black and silvered decorations in the Gothic style. It is a registered design by Wood, dating from 1871. Such designs were common in the 1860s and 1870s, classical motifs having gone out of favour. These mounts were usually approximately one square foot in area

Mourning-cards were also printed in memory of notable personages. Those for Queen Victoria were inscribed with sentiments such as 'The entire world mourns her loss', and those for the prince consort had suitably solemn phrases.

In addition to mourning-stationery, the Victorian Celebration of Death required specially designed tickets for the funerals of the great, illuminated addresses of condolence, and specially printed sheet music. 'Close the Shutters, Willie's Dead', by J. E. Stewart, and 'Little Sister's Gone to Sleep', by C. A. White, were two examples of tear-jerking music of the period, while 'God Bless our Widow Queen', by Passmore and Wrighton, was a popular tribute to Victoria by many an amateur singer; but the more salubrious funeral might well have specially composed anthems sung in the church or cemetery chapel. The Roman Catholic church in England in Victorian days encouraged rich, theatrical, sung Requiem Masses, but the practice declined in Edwardian times.

As well as the expenses of the funeral itself and of the accessories there was, of course, the problem of the erection of a memorial to celebrate the person buried. Mural tablets, often of very pleasing, simple late-classical design, were placed in churches and in the arcades of catacombs. The most usual monument was erected over the actual place of burial. The middle classes purchased freeholds wherever possible, for 'family graves'. These were deep graves, one or two shafts in width, and the coffins were laid on top of one another. Often the most sought-after sites were those on the main avenues of the cemeteries, where brick-lined graves were constructed covered by huge stone slabs over which suitable monuments could be erected. The most ostentatious tombs were the individual family mausolea, where expensive, lead-lined coffins were placed on shelves both above and below ground level in buildings which were secured by massive iron, bronze, or stone doors. These mausolea were in effect small houses, usually big enough for six or eight coffins on either side of a small passage above

[17]

Mausolea in Brookwood Cemetery, near Woking, in Surrey

ground, and sometimes with an underground section as well (above).

However, by far the most common method of disposal of bodies in Victorian times was earth burial, and monuments were erected over the graves. *A Guide to Highgate Cemetery*, by William Justyne, published in London *c* 1865, contains advertisements for monuments by several sculptors who adorned many of the London cemeteries. The advertisements include a sheet of very decent classical monuments by Millward & Co, of 10 Great Russell Street, Bloomsbury, WC (page 19). This firm advertised that they were the only masons who undertook the permanent care of the work they executed.

Cast-iron, wrought-iron, and bronze railings for tomb and grave enclosure were common, and cast iron was also used for monuments, notably Smith's 'Cast-Iron Patent Composite Grave Monuments'. Monumental companies offered 'monuments artistically executed in a sound and substantial manner', and *'immortelles* in great variety'. Photographers offered their services to provide pictures of monuments in the cemeteries, the work to be carried out 'with the utmost care and in the best style'.

Clearly, death in Victorian times was a highly lucrative business. Just as clearly, it was extremely expensive.[8]

Melancholy, Decay, and Romanticism

The wealth of Victorian Britain was made possible not only by internal political security and by pre-eminence in world affairs, but by the nation's lead in manufacture and in food production. The Industrial and Agrarian Revolutions changed the character of the country, and made it an urban society, where display found its greatest numbers of

Designs for tombs. A Victorian advertisement

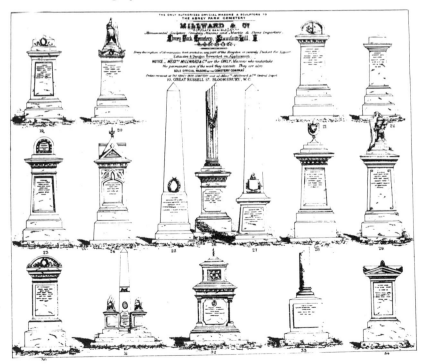

admirers. The customs of Victorian England will be almost beyond comprehension to many people, and this incomprehension, bordering on hostility, tends to be greatest where the art and architecture associated with death are concerned. Yet Victorian expression was perhaps at its most uninhibited in its theatrical treatment of death, and part of the new wealth of society was expended on the funerals and on monuments necessary to establish respectability.

The style of the funeral helped to establish social position, for it was with a funeral, even more than with a wedding, that the wealth and power of a family could be publicly displayed. The vast numbers of relatives and friends, and the expensive flowers, fittings, and coaches fixed the status of a family in the eyes of the onlookers. It also assured the public of the regard in which the deceased was held by the family, for a cheap funeral with no flowers and a plain box for a coffin would have made it clear to the world that the corpse went unloved and unhonoured to its grave. Silver-plated handles of the best quality, a profusion of feathers, and as many trappings as possible became obligatory. The middle and working classes affected the customs of the richer groups, and often ruined themselves in the process.

The Industrial Revolution brought wealth and death. The mortality rates for the first half of the nineteenth century are horrifying, and the dense concentrations of people and the frequency of death made it hard to forget the ephemeral nature of existence. In 1842, for example, the average age at death of a professional man and his family was thirty years, while it was only seventeen for mechanics, labourers, and their families. These figures are taken from the famous *Report on the Sanitary Condition of the Labouring Population of Great Britain*, but they are made rather more melodramatic by the fact that the average included *families*, and, with the high infant mortality rate, the figures are obviously

[20]

affected. As contraception was practically unknown, abortion, murder, and neglect were substituted, and infant mortality compensated for the fecundity of the average Victorian family. Death in childbirth was common, and an epitaph from Folkestone tells a tale that was repeated all over the country:

> Sixteen years a Maiden,
> One twelve Months a Wife,
> One half hour a Mother,
> And then I lost my Life.

The poor lived in conditions that were the subject of concern throughout the century, and yet the rich were not spared frequent visitations from the Angel of Death. We recall that Prince Albert himself died from the effects of bad sanitation. It is therefore not surprising that the Victorians celebrated death. The middle classes and the lower classes buried their dead in the new, hygienic cemeteries, with a panoply which once had been the privilege of the aristocracy alone. Undertakers grew rich, and many firms founded fortunes on the manufacture of enormous quantities of crape. Mourning became deep and prolonged, and was governed by elaborate rules of etiquette. *Immortelles*, stuffed animals and birds, wax flowers, and mementos of the dead became commonplace.

The Victorian Celebration of Death did not just happen. Throughout all cultures and ages death has been regarded as being worthy of some form of ceremonial leave-taking, but the Victorian celebration was something quite unusual because of its scale, throughout all classes of the nation. Never before had the population been so great, and it was still increasing at a phenomenal rate. When Victoria ascended the throne there were only five places in England and Wales outside London with a population of 100,000 or more. In

1800 there had been none. By 1891 there were twenty-three.[9] The number of dead to be buried was enormous, and something very much more satisfactory than the old parish churchyard burial had to be devised, for it must be remembered that what had once been a small village graveyard often had to suffice as a cemetery for the new towns that had grown round the old settlement. Even more unusual, the tender, humanitarian feelings towards the weak and the poor were also felt for the dead. It was a romantic *Zeitgeist* in which these feelings flourished.

In the previous century a perfunctory funeral with all the attendant horrors of overcrowded burial grounds, drunken gravediggers, body-snatchers, the ever-present stench of corruption, and the sight of bones carelessly thrown up from yawning graves had been the normal experience of city dwellers. The Victorians revolted against this, and demanded more secure resting-places for the bodies of their dead where they could visit the graves in pleasant, leafy surroundings without that heartbreaking and common sight of graves lying open again after only a few days, weeks, or months had gone by. Body-snatchers, over-crowded graveyards, and corrupt sextons gave no assurance that a body would rest in peace.

The romantic movement which led to the *Zeitgeist* in which the Victorian Celebration of Death found its full flowering had its source in archaeology and in a delight in decay. There was something about the crumbling parish churches and ruined monasteries of the English landscape that struck an answering chord among the *cognoscenti*. Freed from the imminent threat of Popery, the remains of a Catholic past could be viewed with a kindlier eye. The Gothic atmosphere of Oxford and Cambridge must have contributed to this appreciation, but even more potent were the literary influences which stimulated the romantic

[22]

imagination. We remember Spenser's 'dark, doleful, dreary, greedy grave', and Pope's 'intermingled graves' where 'Black Melancholy' sits, while Mallet's:

Place of Tombs;
Waste, desolate, where *Ruin* dreary dwells,
Brooding o'er sightless Sculls, and crumbling Bones
builds up the imagery of the Gothic graveyard.

It was, however, with Horace Walpole and his 'pretty bauble' of Strawberry Hill that the Gothic Revival really got under way, for Gothic things became highly fashionable. Of course, Walpole was celebrated for the 'Gothic Story' of *The Castle of Otranto*, and his position in society as a man of taste helped to stimulate a real interest in what to those in an Augustan age must have seemed very engaging. Batty Langley's *Gothic Architecture improved by Rules and Proportions in many Grand Designs of Columns, Doors, Windows, Chimney-pieces, Arcades, Colonades, Porticos, Umbrellos, Temples and Pavilions, &c.* was published in 1742 and undoubtedly stirred up much interest, but it was the imagery of the poetry, usually published with a Gothic frontispiece featuring tombs, bones, yews and ruins, that provided the eighteenth century with a heady draught after an age of classical manners and modes.[10]

Polite society, stimulated by literature, by poetry, by the occult, by archaeology, and by high fashion, provided ready subscribers to such weighty tomes as Gough's *Sepulchral Monuments*, and the ever-readable *Gentleman's Magazine*, to which I shall refer many times in the course of this book. By the 1780s and 1790s the subscriber to the *Magazine* could read something about Gothic almost every month. At the turn of the century society became fascinated by the extraordinary building at Fonthill Abbey built for William Beckford by Wyatt; but then Fonthill was primarily scenic display and contrasted with the Gothic of Strawberry Hill.

[*23*]

As scenery, however, it was in the best 'Romantick Landskip' traditions of Shenstone, Repton, and Brown. Romanticism, English landscapes, graves, monuments, and Gothic ruins somehow went together.

The imagery returned again and again to death, the staple food of romantic poetry. The lines

> With solemn delight I survey
> The corpse when the spirit is fled,
> In love with the beautiful clay,
> And longing to lie in its stead[11]

illustrate this.

Yet while society was amusing itself with the sweet smell of decay, and 'melancholy' was a fashionable illness, the population was growing, new manufacturing towns had developed, and the Industrial Revolution was well established. The realisation that there were not enough churches, schools, or burial grounds for the masses was slow to dawn. When it did, Romanticism had given birth to Byronic ideals of freedom, humanitarianism, and compassion for the underdog. The eighteenth century had died with 1789, and, however reluctantly, England saw that things would never be the same. The Augustan Age had passed, but there were survivors from it. The irreligious clerics, the classical churches, the cynicism and rationalism of the period, seemed suddenly to be out of place in the post-Waterloo years. The manners and gallantries of the Regency rakes and their predecessors shocked the rising generation of earnest young people, bred in piety, romanticism and the Englishness of Gothic. The casual way in which the dead were buried; the corrupt practices of sextons and clergy; the hard-boiled rationalism of the eighteenth century—all savoured of the French Jacobinism, of Voltaire, and of godlessness. Christianity was again taken seriously as a bulwark against revolution, and the Church began to recognise the existence of the citizens of the new manu-facturing towns.

Agitation forced the government into action, and when the Church Building Act was passed in 1818, 174 churches were built in a style which came to be known as 'Commissioners' Gothic'. Later, when commentators such as Pugin took up gall-dipped pens for the Gothic cause, buildings became moral issues as well as architectural ones, and it is this profoundly moral attitude, a questioning of the spirit behind the design, that is so illuminating when we consider the Victorians. The earnestness with which the nineteenth-century reformers changed eighteenth-century England was symptomatic of a liberal, enlightened, humanitarian zeal. This attitude changed the physical appearance of British towns and cities, and public buildings began to dominate where once the houses of the rich had done so.[12] Hospitals, schools, churches, railway termini, workhouses, factories, and the huge Victorian cemeteries appeared. The living were to have decent, godly lives; the sick were to be cared for; the poor were to be taken into institutions, however grim; the children were to be educated; and the dead were to be respectfully and reverently buried where they would not be disturbed.

The gin-soaked wrecks who dug the graves in old parish graveyards were to be banished, like Sarah Gamp, and the temporary resting-place of a foul, shallow and insecure grave was to be a thing of the past. Property became within the reach of all enterprising men, and the family grave, like the family house, became a mark of substance. The family, united in life, was to remain so even in death. The Victorian mother, deprived of many of her brood so early, could be comforted by the fact that the frail bodies of her dead children lay securely buried together, and not cast into the parish charnel heap.

[25]

And it was not just the grave itself, but the whole comforting ritual of the funeral which helped to soften the pangs of bereavement. Assured that the soul of someone loved would fly straight to heaven and eternal bliss; fortified by piety, by prayers, and by good works; the Victorian Celebration of Death developed into a customary and ritualistic framework which in itself was an easing activity, affording relief from the horror and grief of bereavement.

In the following chapters the agitation which led to the establishment of the Victorian cemeteries will be discussed, and the formation of the most important of the great nineteenth-century cemeteries will be described. It was only when these spacious cities of the dead had been formed that the Victorian Celebration of Death had full expression, for large and permanent monuments could not be erected in the teeming, overcrowded, and insanitary churchyards. The age required a dignified and beautifully landscaped setting for its dead, and the new cemeteries were worthy of their purpose.

2 Burial, Crisis, Agitation, and Reform

Let's talk of graves, of worms and epitaphs;
Make dust our paper, and with rainy eyes
Write sorrow on the bosom of the earth;
Let's choose executors and talk of wills
William Shakespeare: King Richard II

Burial Customs

The disposal of the dead by earth burial is a very ancient custom. The Bible is full of references to interment as a means of committing cadavers to the elements, and Greek and Roman writings tell us of the funeral customs of the classical period, involving cremation and earth burial. Archaeological evidence has shown that the burial of the dead is a practice almost as old as the history of the human race.

Pagan burial places were always considered to be sacred and set apart. In ancient times burial took place in the fields outside the walls of the towns, for before the advent of Christianity it was not lawful to bring the dead within cities.

During their persecution in Rome under the emperors the Christians buried their martyrs in the Catacombs, and erected altars near the places of burial. After the establishment of the Christian Church the Catacombs were held in reverence for many years. Churches were first erected over or near the places of burial or death of the martyrs, and the next step was to reverse the process and to bury the dead where convenience and growing prosperity caused the erection of churches. Eminent princes and churchmen were buried in the church as a privilege and, as the custom became widespread, the practices of the few were extended to the burials of the many.[1] 'The emanations from the bodies of Saints exercised a peculiar virtue upon all those who lay near them'.[2] Christians inherited the guardianship of the dead, so that cemeteries and churchyards were under the control of the Church, and in later times the clergy became largely dependent upon the fees charged for interment. In 752 St Cuthbert obtained the papal permission to have churchyards added to the churches, and these were surrounded by walls or other barriers, and were consecrated. Consecration by a bishop took the form of a solemn

[28]

procession round the boundaries, expelling by special prayers all evil influences which might disturb the dead. In 1267 Bishop Quevil ordered that all cemeteries in his diocese should be securely enclosed and that no animals should be allowed to graze there.

As the churches themselves became burial grounds, the floors became filled with corpses, and crypts and church-yards became the only possible burial places for pious Christians. Yet the Council of Nantes in the seventh century prohibited burials in the churches, but allowed them in the atrium or in the porticus in special and illustrious cases: *Prohibendum est etiam secundum majorum instituta, ut in ecclesia nullatenus sepeliantur sed in atrio aut porticu aut in exedris ecclesiae.* Despite this ruling, burial continued in the churches, especially of the nobly born, and after a time, particularly in the seventeenth century and afterwards, was fashionable among the more well-to-do members of society. The churchyards became overcrowded, especially when coffins became obligatory.

It appears that 'chesting' or 'boxing' a body in a coffin originated in the attempt to preserve the corpse as long as possible from decay, this being encouraged by Christian belief in a material resurrection. The poor looked upon a coffin as a luxury which sometimes was even denied them by law. To some, until fairly recently, a coffin was the symbol of social status and respectability, and so the undertaker could find in poorer districts a ready demand for polished oak and for ornate coffin furniture. Canon Barnett told of a day's outing to the country for some slum children who were afterwards asked to write essays on their impressions. One little girl was much affected by trees, and described the oak as being the source of '*coffins and other expensive articles*'.[3] 'Chesting' had to take place, of course, when bodies lay in state, or had to travel long distances to

[*29*]

the place of burial. The placing of bodies in coffins made the process of breakdown into the elements very slow, and this process was further retarded when corpses were elaborately buried. Frequently money is found in the coffins, for it was the custom to place coins on the eyes of the dead, a relic of the old superstition that money would be necessary to reach the after-world. Some bodies were buried with a change of clothes, candles, watch and chain, wine and bread, and other items. Others took the precaution of being coffined with a gun, poison, or a knife in case of being prematurely buried. Associated with 'chesting' is the shrouding of corpses, a very ancient custom involving materials as varied as barks of trees, matting, animal skins or furs, linen, flannel, silk and costly clothes. Alexander Pope commented upon the compulsory shrouding of bodies in wool, an enactment which was made in order to bolster up the declining national industry in 1666. In *Moral Essays* we find the lines:

'Odious! in woollen! 'twould a saint provoke,'
(Were the last words that poor Narcissa spoke)
'No, let a charming chintz and Brussels lace
Wrap my cold limbs, and shade my lifeless face'[4]

This story, according to Pope, is founded on fact. 'Several attribute this in particular to a very celebrated actress [Mrs Oldfield], who, in detestation of the thought of being buried in woollen, gave these her last orders with her dying breath.' The law of 1666 was easily and frequently evaded, for in the year 1678 and again in 1680 it was amended; a provision was added that a certificate must be given by the relative of the deceased, in the form of an affidavit, declaring that a woollen shroud had been used. The law helped the paper trade, for as a result 200,000lb of rag were saved from the grave. A heavy fine was imposed

[*30*]

for non-compliance, and the parish churches were obliged to keep a special register of burials. The affidavit was made before a JP or a clergyman that the law had been complied with. The laws were not repealed until 1814.

The taking of money, food, and drink into the afterworld is but a shadow of the old customs, once prevalent throughout the world, of taking concubines, slaves, horses, jesters, and servants to the grave. We recall that *suttee* in India was not abolished until 1829, and the practice may have continued long after that. Relics of such customs still remain with us, such as when the widow follows behind the coffin or when a riderless charger is led behind the hearse of a great national figure. Once, the widow and horse would have been slaughtered at the grave. Herodotus tells us that often horses were maimed so that the unfortunate animals might appear to be grief-stricken, while the Turks used to put mustard seed in horses' nostrils so that they would appear to weep.

Watching of the dead occurs in Celtic lands today, and in ancient Jewish practice. Jewish dead were placed in a sepulchre which remained unsealed for three days, during which period the body was visited by relatives in the hope that signs of a return to life would be found. We recall such a visit on that first Easter morning, so long ago. In Celtic custom, however, the 'wake' is held at the home, and not at the sepulchre, but this is probably for climatic reasons. Paid 'watchers' became common in Britain at one time.

As we have seen, the custom of general burial inside the church appears to have grown from the sixteenth century. The early Christians regarded dead bodies as unclean, but the fashion for burial inside the church grew generally in Europe. The churches of Delft and Amsterdam, for example, have floors entirely composed of vault covers. When William of Orange became King William III, Netherlandish practice became fashionable in Britain. Churches became filled with monuments to those lying beneath the floor. Evelyn records that his father-in-law decreed that he should be buried in the churchyard, 'he being much offended by the novel custom of burying everyone within the body of the church and chancel, that being a favour heretofore granted to the martyrs and great persons, the excess of making churches charnel-houses being of ill and irreverent example and prejudicial to the health of the living, besides the continual disturbance of the pavement and seats, and several other indecencies . . .'5 The maxim of the worthy old gentleman might well have been 'The churchyard for the dead—the church for the living'. Dr William Wynne composed his own epitaph which he caused to be erected in Mold church, in Flintshire. It read:

> In conformity to an ancient usage,
> From a proper regard to decency,
> And a concern for the health
>   of his fellow-creatures,
> He was moved to give particular directions
> for being buried in the adjoining church-yard,
>   and not in the church.

These lines are quoted in Joseph Taylor's *The Danger of Premature Interment*.6

The Church has sometimes refused burial in the churchyards, not only to unbaptised children, suicides, and lunatics, but also to excommunicated persons. In early medieval times a gate was erected at the entrance to churchyards where those who were in fact entitled to burial in the churchyard could have the first part of the service read. The gates are known as lich-gates, or lych-gates, from a Saxon word related to the German *Leiche*, meaning 'corpse'.

[*32*]

Crisis and Agitation

By Stuart times churchyards in the towns were grossly overcrowded. Evelyn describes them as being 'filled up with earth, or rather the congestion of dead bodies one above the other, to the very top of the walls, and some above the walls, so that the churches seemed to be built in pits'.[7] The City of London churchyards are often much higher than street level, and often even country churchyards form a ridge round the building.

The chaos may be imagined when plague made its regular visitation. In 1349, in respect of a plague and infection, thirteen acres and a rood of land adjoining 'No-man's land', lying in a place called 'Spittle Croft' [because it belonged to St Bartholomew's Hospital] were purchased for burial. It is clear from contemporary records that even in such dreadful days the Church saw to it that cemeteries were enclosed by walls and duly consecrated in accordance with Christian custom.

As London and other cities expanded in medieval times and the gardens became built over, the old parish grave-yards had excessive demands placed on them. In order to meet this demand, ossuaries or charnel houses were erected to which the bones of the dead were removed to make way for new interments. Most of these ossuaries were cleared in the sixteenth and seventeenth centuries, and the last great clearance for the new cemeteries was effected in the nineteenth century.

Space was limited, and the overcrowding was aggravated by plague and by other epidemics. Stow tells us of the plague in London increasing 'so sore' that, from want of room in churchyards to bury the dead of the city and suburbs, John Corey, clerk, purchased of Nicholas Prior of the Holy Trinity, Aldgate, one loft of ground near East Smithfield for the burial of the dead, with condition that it might be called the Churchyard of the Holy Trinity, which several devout citizens enclosed by a wall of stone. From the same source we learn that the Bishop of London bought a piece of land called 'No-man's land', which he enclosed with a wall of brick and dedicated to the burial of the dead, building on it a chapel which was later enlarged and made into a dwelling. The burial ground became a fair garden retaining the old name of 'Pardon Churchyard'. This was a foretaste of things to come.[8]

The 'sweating sickness' of 1551 attacked the British Isles with devastating effect, but it was not until 1665 that some real organisation seems to have been formed to deal with the problem of disposing of large numbers of corpses in London. The City was divided into districts, each with nurses, watchers, and gravediggers, and regulations were enforced to protect the survivors. The City Fathers drew up rules for the burial of the dead by the visitation. Burial was to be before sunrise or before sunset, within the jurisdiction of the churchwardens or constable. No neighbours or friends were to accompany the corpse to church, or to enter the house 'visited', upon pain of imprisonment or having their houses shut up. No corpse dying of infection was to be buried, or to remain in, any church in time of common prayer, sermon or lecture; no children were to go near a corpse, coffin or grave in a church, churchyard or burying-place; all graves were to be at least six feet deep; and all public assemblies at burials were to be discontinued during the time of the plague. All houses which the plague had visited were to be marked with a red cross one foot in length on the middle of the door, and the words 'Lord have mercy on us' were to be inscribed. It was not until the following year, when the Great Fire destroyed the accumulated filth of old London, that the great danger of bubonic plague was radically reduced, but clearly the precautions taken over burials showed that the authorities were starting to think seriously about the problems of disposing of dead bodies.

It had become apparent that some radical and hygienic method of disposing of the dead should be adopted. The state of the churchyards, especially in London, was deplorable in the seventeenth century, and John Evelyn campaigned for the formation of cemeteries outside the City after the Plague and Fire. It was not until the nineteenth century, however, that any major reforms were made, although the Dissenters had formed their own model cemetery at Bunhill Fields much earlier.[9] Sir Christopher Wren had proposed cemeteries situated in the outskirts of towns where beautiful monuments could be erected, but yet the dimensions should be regulated by an architect and not left to the fancy of every mason. He said 'I could wish all burials in churches and churchyards might be disallowed . . .'[10] Indeed, an article in *The Builder* of 1843 contrasted the 'wisdom of Wren, against the puerilities of Pugin'.[11] This was a reference to the fact that Pugin favoured churchyards and church burial because of their religious significance. The same journal thundered that London 'stores and piles up 50,000 of its dead, to putrefy, to rot, to give out exhalations, to darken the air with vapours . . . 50,000 desecrated corpses each year stacked in some 150 limited pits of churchyards',[12] and quoted a letter by G. A. Walker, surgeon, on the condition of the churchyards.

The rationalists of the seventeenth and eighteenth centuries agitated, but without much success. Evelyn wrote that it was a pity the churchyards had not been banished to the north walls of the City, where a gated enclosure, of competent breadth, for a mile in length, might have served for a universal cemetery to all the parishes. These walls

[35]

would be adorned with monuments, inscriptions, and titles, apt for contemplation and memory of the dead. Perhaps Bunhill Fields might be regarded as a very small-scale model of what Evelyn had in mind.

The Dissenters' burial ground at Bunhill Fields was in many ways a model for what was to come in the nineteenth century. Timbs, in his *Curiosities of London*,[13] states that the name derives from a deposit of more than 1,000 cartloads of bones removed from the charnel-houses of old St Paul's in Elizabeth I's reign. He reports that in 1553 a lease was granted to the Corporation of London together with other lands. It was apparently used for recreation purposes, but by 1665 it had become a burial place.[14] In Maitland's *Survey* it is stated that 'part whereof at present denominated Tindal's or the Dissenters' burial-ground, was by the Mayor and Corporation of London, in the year 1665, set apart and consecrated as a common cemetery' for the interment of such corpses as could not have room in the burial grounds in the dreadful year of the pestilence. However, it not being made use of on that occasion, 'the said Tindal took a lease thereof, and converted it into a burial-ground'. The name *Bon-hill* or *Bone-Hill* probably dates from the mid-sixteenth century, although the first burial there as such appears to have been in 1665.

Edmund Curll published a register of burials in Bunhill Fields in 1717, and showed evidence therein that the graves were sold in perpetuity, and that any attempt to sell the soil for secular purposes would be desecration.[15] It is fascinating to note that Bunhill Fields was in fact conserved in the 1860s. What actually happened was that, although it had always been understood that the Dissenters' Burial Ground was to remain for ever intact, it fell into the hands of the Ecclesiastical Commissioners. The result was the setting up of a committee, who agitated for the conservation of the graveyard not only on religious grounds, but as a singularly rich burial ground with fine monuments and sculptures. On 16 November 1865 the Court of Common Council learned with regret that the Ecclesiastical Commissioners had no disposition to concur in an arrangement for the preservation of the Bunhill Fields' Burial Ground, except upon terms of sale and purchase. The Court noted the antiquity of the spot as a place of extramural sepulture; that it had been held by the Corporation for more than five hundred years; that it had been set apart and used for centuries as a place of interment; that a public pledge had been given by the conjoint authorisation of the Ecclesiastical authorities and the Corporation that the ground should at all times remain for the purposes of burials only, and that up to the year 1832, upon these conditions and assurances, vaults had been sold. The Court protested against the application of the ground or any part of it to secular uses, and, considering the historic interest attaching to the Bunhill Fields Burial Ground in consequence of the interment of so many distinguished and honoured men of all creeds and parties, the Court was willing to accept the care and preservation of the ground on behalf of the public, and to assist in promoting any well-advised scheme for securing against molestation and disturbance the final resting-place of so many thousands of their fellow citizens. It was ordered that a copy of the resolutions be transmitted to the Ecclesiastical Commissioners.

The result was an Act of Parliament to maintain the cemetery, but to allow the public access to it. No fragment of stone was to be removed, and careful tending would be the policy. As a policy it deserves the highest praise. The *Proceedings in Reference to the Preservation of Bunhill Fields Burial ground with Inscriptions on the Tombs* was published in London in 1867. It contains Edmund Curll's *Inscriptions* reprinted. The members of the Corporation of London undertook the conservancy of Bunhill Fields Burial Ground on condition that it was placed in their hands as trustees for the public. The names of those far-sighted men should be recorded: Charles Reed was their chairman, and the committee consisted of J. C. Lawrence, B. Bower, B. Burnell, R. N. Phillipps, G. R. Longden, J. Sewell, A. S. Ridley, G. J. Cockerell, S. Gibbins, J. Richardson, and H. H. Heath.[16]

It was only to be expected that the radical idea of establishing a large cemetery was first carried out by Dissenters, for the reason that burial in the old churchyards was associated with the Established Church and also with popery, and therefore was distasteful. The Church could deny burial in consecrated ground to Dissenters, while they, in turn, were in no mind to be buried in such ground. Besides, the whole vexed question of payment of burial fees to the Established Church caused a great deal of trouble. It was obviously felt that separate burial grounds were essential. The significance of Bunhill Fields is enormous, and the character of the place is of immense importance as a relic of a complete period where the taste of that society was expressed in the design of tombstones. The splendid seventeenth-century monuments are pleasing to the eye and the over-all atmosphere and visual quality of the place is very fine indeed (page 69).[17]

Among those buried there is Thomas Goodwin, who attended Cromwell on his deathbed. Bunyan lies in the vault of his friend Strudwick, the grocer of Holborn. Edmund Curll does not record Bunyan's name, but the inscription was added later. Southey tells us that people liked to be buried in company, and in good company. 'The Dissenters regarded Bunhill Fields as their Campo Santo.' Fleetwood, Cromwell's son-in-law, is buried there, as are

John Dunton, Daniel Defoe, Daniel Williams, Rev D. Neal, and Susannah Wesley, mother of John and Charles Wesley. Near the centre is a monument to Isaac Watts. Also here were buried William Blake, Thomas Stothard and that Thomas Hardy who was tried for treason with John Horne Tooke.

There were others, of course, who saw that the existing churchyards were wholly inadequate and had long since been filled. The Reverend Thomas Lewis, writing in 1721,[18] could give us his *Seasonable Considerations on the Indecent and Dangerous Custom of BURYING in Churches and Churchyards, with remarkable OBSERVATIONS historical and philosophical. Proving that the Custom is not only contrary to the Practice of the Antients, but fatal, in case of INFECTION.* He gave sensible warnings as well as ecclesiastical arguments; for example, he asked if we could believe 'that the Carcasses of the Dead which polluted the Temples before, can give them Consecration now, which is inverting the Nature of Things'. Mr Lewis demonstrated that 'the BURYING of the DEAD in CHURCHES and CHURCHYARDS may be prejudicial to the LIVING', and pointed out that the 'Doctrine of the MASS was invented . . . to compleat the Cheat, that is, to bring SUPERSTITION to its Zenith, and perfect the Design of enriching the Coffers of the POPE and CLERGY . . . And therefore, those places where, or near to which the Mass was celebrated, were preferable to all other, and no Cost was to be spared for the obtaining so great a Benefit.' Another reason, according to him, for burying in churches was 'GAIN and LUCRE'.[19]

Some Literary References

Literature is full of references to burial customs, to funerals, and to the state of burial grounds at various periods in history.

P. H. Ditchfield, in *The Old-time Parson*, describes Stoke
Poges churchyard as a neglected spot, and of a London
churchyard he quotes from Webb's *Collection of Epitaphs*:[20]

> Here nauseous weeds each pile surround,
> And things obscene bestrew the ground;
> Sculls, bones, in moulding fragments lie,
> All dreadful emblems of mortality.

Certainly, in Georgian days the churchyards had sunk to
absolute chaos. Added to the obscenities of overcrowded
burial grounds were the activities of the resurrection men.
It was therefore in the eighteenth century that the churchyards became surrounded by massive iron railings, and
individual graves were covered by huge slabs of stone, or
even by altar-tombs.

Charles Dickens left us a wonderful description of the
City of London churchyards in *The Uncommercial Traveller*.
'Such strange churchyards hide in the City of London;
churchyards sometimes so entirely detached from churches,
always so pressed upon by houses; so small, so rank, so
silent, so forgotten, except by the few people who ever look
down into them from their smoky windows.' He also
described the churchyard of 'Saint Ghastly Grim', with a
'ferocious strong spiked iron gate' and ornamented with
skulls and cross-bones, 'wrought in stone'. These skulls
'grin aloft horribly, thrust through and through with iron
spears'. The gate is that at the entrance to the churchyard of
St Olave, Hart Street, which gives us some idea of the scale
and feeling of a London churchyard, although now it is only
used by City workers as a little park.[21]

Dickens described many of the London burial grounds,
and he gives a vivid account of one in Chapter Sixteen of
Bleak House. 'By many devious ways', he wrote, 'reeking
with offence of many kinds, they came to the little tunnel

of a court, and to the gas-lamp (lighted now), and to the iron gate. "He was put there", says Jo, holding to the bars and looking in. "Where?" O, what a scene of horror!

' "There!" says Jo, pointing. "Over yinder. Among them piles of bones, and close to that there kitchen winder! They put him wery nigh the top. They was obliged to stamp upon it to git it in. I could unkiver it for you with my broom, if the gate was open. That's why they locks it, I s'pose", giving it a shake. "It's always locked. Look at the rat!" cries Jo, excited. "Hi! look! There he goes! Ho! Into the ground!" ' The question is asked in *Bleak House* if such a place of abomination could be consecrated. The description could have fitted many churchyards of the eighteenth and nineteenth centuries.[22]

Such imagery from the past is powerful, and affects us with a strange melancholy. Inseparable from the picture of an old burial ground is the planting of trees and shrubs. Yews, cypresses, and weeping willows spring to mind, of course, as do box and cedar. Abraham bought a field on the death of Sarah, but he was not satisfied until 'the cave that was therein and all the trees that were in the field, that were in all the borders round about, were made sure'.[23] Tree-worship was associated with ancient burial places; and certain trees, such as oak and ash, rowan and mistletoe, were associated with power against evil spirits. The churchyard was also the arsenal in ancient times, and the yew provided the bows for the armies. Trees also helped to dry the soil and to protect the church from wind, as well as providing shelter in the churchyard. Gasquet, in *Parish Life in Mediaeval England*, tells us that trees in churchyards were grown by the clergy in order to provide timber for the repair work to the churches. Trees could clearly help to absorb certain chemicals deposited by decomposing corpses, and so there was an additional reason for such planting. Symbolism must have played its part as well, and old beliefs indicate that the roots of the yew would find and stop the mouths of the dead. The weeping willow has an obvious affinity with mourning, but it also is significant in that it properly derives its life from streams and rivers, and so was accepted as a symbol of resurrection, and its branches are borne by mourners at masonic funerals. The cypress was a Roman symbol of mourning, while rosemary and box were tokens of remembrance. The palm was the symbol of peace, and also of victory over death. Indeed, the palm frond is often depicted in the Catacombs in Rome. Mandrakes were credited with personalities of their own, possibly because they resemble the human form, having two taproots which are akin to the lower limbs. When a mandrake is pulled from the ground, a sound is produced which resembles a shriek. *Get with child a mandrake root* is clearer when we consider the symbolism.

The first fruits of agitation

As the nineteenth century progressed, the graveyards became more and more overcrowded. In Paris new cemeteries had been laid out, and those became models for other countries. As they became adorned by grand monuments, their virtues were so celebrated that certain books of designs were published, among them *Monumens Funéraires Choisis Dans Les Cimetières de Paris et des Principales Villes de France*, by Normand Fils, 1832,[24] and *Les Principaux Monuments Funéraires Du Père-Lachaise, de Montmartre, du Mont-Parnasse et autres Cimetières de Paris Dessinés et Mesurés par Rousseau, architecte et Lithographiés par Lassalle, Accompagnés d'une Description succincte du monument et d'une Notice historique sur le personnage qu'il renferme*, by Marty, in 1840.[25] Other volumes, such as *The Danger of Premature Interment Proved from Many Remarkable Instances of People who have recovered after being laid out for dead and of others entombed alive for want of being properly*

[42]

examined prior to Interment by Joseph Taylor, published in 1816; an *Essay on Sepulchres*, published in London in 1809;[26] and various pamphlets roused articulate opinion, so that the climate was ripe for the establishment of the large cemeteries in London.

Other cities had pioneered the formation of large or fairly large cemeteries away from the centres of cities. One of the earliest was Belfast, which had no less than two fine cemeteries, one for the Roman Catholics and one for the Protestants. The old graveyard at Carlisle Circus, Belfast, was largely founded by radical thinkers at the turn of the century. The tombstone of Dr Young sums up the rather revolutionary nature of a body of men who were far in advance of their contemporaries in London at that time in terms of carrying out much needed reforms (below).

'Young! moulders here 1829' *Dr Young's grave in the old cemetery at Carlisle Circus, Belfast*

The humorous yet realistic attitude presented by Dr Young's gravestone is the antithesis of the sanctimonious expressions

'St James's Cemetery in Liverpool had been laid out between 1825 and 1829 in the quarries above which Scott's mighty Anglican cathedral now towers.' The architect was John Foster

of sentimentality found on many eighteenth- and nineteenth-century monuments.

Liverpool was among the first cities in Britain to establish a cemetery. St James's Cemetery was created from a disused stone quarry during the years 1825-9 at a cost of £21,000. It was for many years the chief burial place of Liverpudlians. The architect was John Foster who made a dramatic setting for this great necropolis. Huge ramps were constructed with paths to convey the funerals to the sunken floor of the cemetery. Catacombs were hollowed into its stone walls, and tunnels were hollowed out of the solid rock to provide awe-inspiring settings for the interment of the dead (page 44). The power and scale of this cemetery were immense, and it had a most macabre effect as it mouldered in the damp atmosphere. Unfortunately it has undergone a transformation which was commenced in 1969, and it has lost much of its atmosphere and robust character. The mortuary chapel was a gem of the Greek Revival; pure and diminutive. Among the monuments is the little circular mausoleum of the Member of Parliament, William Huskisson, who was killed while assisting at the inauguration of the Liverpool & Manchester Railway. It has a dome over fluted Corinthian columns, and is surmounted by a cross. It was designed by Foster, and contains a statue of the MP by the celebrated John Gibson. This cemetery frequently features in *In Memoriam, or, Funeral Records of Liverpool Celebrities*.[27] This curious volume gives an astonishingly rich picture of nineteenth-century funerals, some very rich, and some very simple. Familiar phrases such as 'coffins of finest oak with gilt furnishings and brass handles' and 'the Undertakers undertook the entire management of the ceremonial proceedings' occur with regularity. The architectural grandeur of St James's Cemetery is heightened by the mighty Anglican Cathedral, designed by Sir Giles Gilbert

[45]

The Glasgow necropolis

Scott in the Gothic style, which towers above the cemetery.

When Lord Lansdowne moved that interment within London was highly objectionable, leading to consequences injurious to health and offensive to decency, he pointed out that Liverpool possessed a large cemetery 'erected under the care of Mr Foster, a distinguished architect', and that it was 'highly approved of by the people there.'[28]

Glasgow also led with the formation of its necropolis in 1832. East of the Cathedral and separated from it by the Molendinar ravine, the cemetery is constructed on a rocky eminence rising 225ft above the level of the Clyde. Entrance to this magnificent necropolis is gained by the bridge that spans the ravine, appropriately termed 'The Bridge of Sighs'. The ground was bought in 1650 by the Merchants' House, and the cemetery was laid out with the intention of modelling it on Père-la-Chaise in Paris. The

[46]

original proposal to form a necropolis on the site was made by Dean of Guild James Ewing, later Provost and MP, and he was supported by Laurence Hill, the collector, and by Dr John Strang, the chamberlain. Strang was to declare that he was solely actuated by the desire of awakening the attention of his countrymen to the generally neglected condition of the churchyards. Contemporary opinions of the necropolis were favourable, the scheme being considered 'magnificent', but it was feared it would not be patronised by Glaswegians. An Edinburgh newspaper anticipated the time when the citizens of that city would turn their attentions to similar improvements. Dr Strang was described as a 'brilliant super-orthodox luminary burning in a dense cloud of Scotch prejudice and Glasgow smoke'.

It was originally intended to drive a tunnel through the hill with catacombs off it, but this plan was abandoned. Instead, Egyptian Vaults were constructed, the site was surrounded by a wall, and secured by stout gates. The gate-keeper's lodge was not erected until 1839. The ground is intersected by several walks and drives, and these are bordered by monumental erections of beautiful design. One of the oldest and most conspicuous is a Doric column surmounted by a twelve-foot-high figure of John Knox, erected in 1824. Among the most notable of the monuments are those to Sheridan Knowles, the dramatist; to Michael Scott, author; to William Miller, author of *Wee Willie Winkie*; to Edward Irving; and to William Motherwell, the poet. The Jew's Sepulchre at the north end of the grounds is interesting architecturally, and it was there that the first interment took place. As the necropolis is built on solid rock, the graves, or 'lairs', as they are termed, are cut into the stone and covered with hinged slabs. From afar, the necropolis is a dreamlike vision of Attic splendour, almost unbelievable in the context of Glasgow (pages 46 and 48).

[47]

The Glasgow necropolis

In a description of the Glasgow Necropolis, we read that 'amid the green glades and gloomy cypresses which surround and overshadow the vast variety of sepulchral monuments of Père-la-Chaise, the contemplative mind is not only impressed with sentiments of solemn sublimity and religious awe, but with those of the most tender and heart-affecting melancholy'. The author describes the natural drying of bodies in certain conditions, quoting the vaults of Bremen, of Vienna, and of Palermo as affording examples of natural desiccation.[29]

The great John Claudius Loudon visited the Glasgow Necropolis in 1842, and wrote up his experiences in *The Gardener's Magazine*, of which he was editor. 'The impression . . . is grand and melancholy.' An archway leads to the 'Necropolis, or ornamented Public Cemetery, constructed by the Merchants' House of Glasgow, in their property, to supply the accommodation required by a rapidly increasing population, and, by embellishing the place of sepulture, to invest with more soothing associations that affectionate recollection of the departed which is cherished by those who survive'.[30] Loudon was to publish a treatise on cemetery design in *The Gardener's Magazine* the following year.[31]

Such new cemeteries captured the imaginations of the reformers. France was seen as providing the example, and writers of all description, from hack journalists to famous poets, took up their pens in the cause of the new, hygienic cemeteries which had been pioneered on the European continent.

Washington Irving advised that there was no need to surround cemeteries with unnecessary horrors, and Coleridge suggested nature should be brought into cemeteries, with planting and imaginative use of trees. Coleridge warned that, in our anxiety to escape from gloom and horror, we must not run into the opposite extreme of meretricious gaudiness. The new British cemeteries were to bear a solemn and soothing character, equally remote from fanatical gloom and from conceited affectation.[32]

It was, however, the redoubtable Mr G. F. Carden who can take most of the credit for the moulding of opinion so that the great cemeteries could be created. George Frederick Carden was a Barrister-at-Law, with chambers at 3 Inner Temple Lane. The *Penny Magazine* had for years given Mr Carden great coverage in his campaign to improve the burial grounds of Britain, which were contrasted with those of other civilised nations. 'Seek the abodes of the dead in France, Spain, Germany, or in the principal States of America, and in place of the hideous burial-grounds described . . . we find open and airy places, mostly decent, frequently beautiful' was Carden's advice. Instead of sending away in disgust the few whom sad necessity had made their visitors, the new cemeteries often formed the favourite places of resort for the neighbouring population. France had honourably distinguished herself in this matter, for not content with stopping the old custom, and prescribing the strictest sanitary laws for the future, she purified her metropolis of the evils already in existence by the Herculean task of removing the enormous masses of human remains which had been congregated there to the famous Catacombs of Paris, where now lie the bones of at least three million people. Carden contrasted the practices of London, which were put to shame even by the provincial towns; Liverpool and Manchester having had their cemeteries for years before London seems to have paid the slightest attention to the problem.[33]

New Orleans had been forced to approach the problem in an unusual way, constructing its cemeteries so that the bodies were deposited *above* ground since the water table was so high. This led to the development of a funeral art unequalled in the United States of America. Plastered brick buildings painted with whitewash housed narrow receptacles for the dead, the entrances being sealed with memorial tablets. By 1820 stone was being used for pediments and ornament, despite the fact that stone had to be imported to the city. Costs were high, however, and brick, wood, and iron were the cheapest materials for tombs, although they did not last well in the swampy cemeteries. Stone was used for sculpture, and it is in the cemeteries that the best stonework in New Orleans is found, dating from 1840 to 1875, after which quality declined, feeling being lost and monotony resulting. The Girod Street Cemetery in New Orleans had *loculi* that were rented out to the poorer families for a limited time, the bones then being cleared out. This cemetery for Protestants, in use before 1820, is the strangest in the USA and the oldest in New Orleans. The St Roch Cemetery was completely surrounded by a thick wall containing tiers of *loculi* somewhat resembling bakers' ovens.

The St Louis Cemetery had many Creole tombs of extravagant design.[34]

Thomas Miller, in his *Picturesque Sketches of London Past and Present*,[35] felt that amid the din and tumult of a populous city the dead were sadly misplaced. He could never look upon those close unhealthy corners, crowded with graves, without feeling that it was wrong to bury the dead there; that they ought to be removed from such shadowy and sunless spots to where the tall trees would make a 'soothing murmur' above their heads, and all around them be 'gentle images of rest'. Their business with this world was ended; they had finished their 'long day's work'; the roll of carriages, the tramp of busy passengers, and living voices, clamorous for gain, ever sounded harshly in his ear when they came grating and jarring amongst the resting-places of the dead. 'The price of corn, the state of the money-market, or the rising and falling of the funds', he wrote, 'are matters which ought to be discussed far away from those we followed, and wept over, and consigned to their silent chambers, there to sleep till the last trumpet sounds.' Mr Miller contrasted this with his view of the open cemetery, where it would be possible to walk through a land littered with living affections, and strewn over with tokens of existing love. There, sympathies would be divided between the mourned and the mourners, for sorrow is not alone for the dead; the flowers would be reminders of those people who went to the cemetery now and then to weep, and to remember.

The sentiments of the day are expressed in Mr Miller's resounding claim that against the unhealthy graveyards, sentence had been pronounced; they were doomed to be closed. It was useless for selfish and mercenary men to oppose the fiat which had gone forth, for the air of the city had too long been poisoned through men who lived by the dead. 'Let us create a good out of this evil; and after these unhealthy churchyards have been closed long enough to destroy the injurious exhalations which have of late numbered so many of the living with the dead, then let the grounds be planted with trees and flowers, and they will become sweet breathing-places, like our squares, and amid the brick walls call up images of the far-away country.[36] The old monuments need not be disturbed. To see the drooping branches of a green tree falling over them, will add to their beauty and solemnity; and in the centre of our cities we can wander among groves rendered sacred by the remains of our forefathers . . .' Clearly, the romantic period created imagery of powerful appeal to writers on the topic. They could hardly have foreseen the dreary acres of late nineteenth-century cemeteries or their hideous twentieth-century equivalent. For the time, the dead in the overcrowded city churchyards were:

> very mild and meek;
> Though [sextons] smite them on the cheek
> And on the mouth—they cannot speak.

and

> They hear not [Poor-law guardians] rave,
> Nor moaning household shelter crave
> (When carted from each thrice-sold grave).

Mr Miller's zeal and enthusiasm knew no bounds when he described the new dream cemeteries. Open cheap cemeteries, and conveyances thither, would spring up rapidly enough; funeral omnibuses would be started at cheap fares. If nothing else would suffice, Mr Miller demanded that society be rated for burying the dead, for it did not murmur at supporting them while living, nor should it begrudge the slight tax that would be required for interring them in surburban cemeteries. 'There are thousands of acres of land

[52]

to be sold within five miles of the City of London; if we go to the distance of ten miles it will be all the better for our children's children; but let no buildings be erected within a measured mile of these Silent Cities of the Dead, but each for ever remain a Great Garden of Graves.'

Affection, said Mr Miller, would often visit the Land of the Dead; the widow would take her children by the hand, and lead them into the cemetery, and shew them the little freehold in which their father slept. The poor would become more pious, and amid their troubles thank God that they had at last a tranquil haven, in which they could for ever moor their storm-tossed barques: to them suburban cemeteries would become spots filled with solemn associations—homes to which they were 'fast hastening' with patient resignation.[37]

The literature of the period is full of such fulsome panegyrics on the cemetery. Undoubtedly, much of the pro-cemetery lobby was influenced by a romantic *Zeitgeist*, but there were obvious reasons why the churchyards should be closed and new, larger, burial grounds should be established. If any crises arose, such as cholera epidemics, of which there were several in the first half of the nineteenth century, the churchyards became scenes of the most appalling horror, where bones would be heaped on bones, and partially rotted bodies would be disinterred to make way for a multitude of corpses. Since premature disinterment was common practice anyway, it was clear that something had to be done in order that death could be celebrated in a hygienic and dignified manner in surroundings more fitting than the loathsome corruption of the churchyards. Elysium and Arcady were to be the ideals, where memorials to the dead standing among pastoral landscapes created in the best traditions of English classical design would give solace to the bereaved.

[53]

3 The first great metropolitan cemetery in Britain

For there is good news yet to hear and fine things to be seen,
Before we go to Paradise by way of Kensal Green.
            G. K. Chesterton: The Rolling English Road

A MEETING WAS convened by G. F. Carden on 8 February 1830 for the purpose of ascertaining the best mode of improving the system of burial in the metropolis. The original provisional committee included Carden, Andrew Spottiswoode MP, and Robert Sievier. This meeting was recorded on page 1 of the minutes of the General Cemetery Company, and it was from this gathering of enthusiasts that the first large cemetery in London developed as a reality.

J. C. Loudon wrote to the *Morning Advertiser* on 14 May 1830. His letter shows that he was in at the beginning on the problems of cemetery design:

Sir,

Observing by the reports from the Commons House in this day's paper, that the above subject is likely soon to undergo discussion, allow me to suggest that there should be several burial-grounds, all, as far as practicable, equi-distant from each other, and from what may be considered the centre of the metropolis; that they be regularly laid out and planted with every sort of hardy trees and shrubs; and that in interring the ground be used on a plan similar to that adopted in the burial-ground of Munich, and not left to chance like Père la Chaise [*sic*]. These and every other burial-ground in the country, might be made, at no expense whatever, botanic gardens; for, were nurserymen and gardeners invited, I am certain they would supply, every one to his own parish, gratis, as many hardy trees and shrubs, and herbaceous plants, as room could be found for. It would be for the clergy and the vestries to be at the expense of rearing these trees if they choose, which I think they ought to do, if they get them for nothing.

The burial-places for the metropolis ought to be made sufficiently large to serve at the same time as breathing places, and most churchyards in the country are now too

[55]

small for the increased population. To accomplish the above and other metropolitan improvements properly, there ought to be a standing commission, for the purpose of taking into consideration whatever might be suggested for the general improvement, not only of London, but of the environs.

J. C. L.

Bayswater, May 14, 1830

That Loudon should have given so much thought to his particular theories concerning cemeteries, botanic gardens, and the recreational possibilities of cemeteries is of great interest, for he did not actually publish his classic work on cemeteries until 1843.

The *Morning Chronicle* of Thursday, 10 June 1830 reported that a public meeting had been held at the Freemasons' Tavern, with Lord Milton in the chair. It was proposed to form a large cemetery because the manner in which bodies of the dead were disposed of in the metropolis had long been a subject of complaint. The company was to be called 'The General Cemetery Company', and shares would not be capable of being transferred until three-fifths of the amount had been paid up. Discussion took place about compensation to clergy if a vested interest existed, and about the benefits of a new cemetery reducing the expense of interment. It was reported that the Bishop of London supported the idea. G. F. Carden was specifically mentioned as the projector of the plan.[1]

The founders of The General Cemetery Company had discussed various sites in the late 1820s, and in 1830 the Eyre Estate and Primrose Hill were seriously considered as a possible location for London's first great cemetery. G. F. Carden was highly active in propaganda work in 1830, and a petition was made to Parliament by Andrew Spottiswoode MP. The first trustees of the company were Spottiswoode, Carden, Viscount Milton, and Sir John Dean Paul. In July 1831 land was purchased at Kensal Green, just off the Harrow Road, in what was then a completely rural landscape. In 1832 the company secured an Act of Parliament to facilitate its activities, and a board of directors was appointed. *The British Almanac* for 1883, pp218-19, stated that 'An Act of Parliament having been obtained last session incorporating a company for the purpose of providing a place of burial removed from the population of the metropolis, a large plot of ground has been purchased at Kensal Green, lying north-west of London, a little beyond Paddington'. This ground was enclosed, and a temporary chapel was erected, so that it could be immediately applied to the purpose of sepulture, before the more permanent buildings were undertaken.

Many architects were interested in the problems of cemetery design, and many produced speculative schemes both for commercial and academic reasons. In 1827 Pugin had exhibited a design for an entrance gateway to a cemetery at the Royal Academy. In February 1830 Benjamin Wyatt was invited to be the architect to the company. He declined, but recommended Charles Fowler, who joined the committee that year, as did Pugin himself. On 9 June there was a communication from Francis Goodwin, who had hopes of becoming the architect. He described his designs for a public cemetery sited on Primrose Hill which he trusted would interest the General Cemetery Company. These drawings, now in the Soane Museum, were described in the *Gentleman's Magazine*[2] as being prepared by an architect of some celebrity who conceived the plan of making the cemetery 'a very magnificent display of architecture'. The committee was also approached by Thomas Willson with a view to having his plans for a pyramid cemetery exhibited in 1824 adopted, but Willson reported the failure of this in

[57]

July 1831. It was decided that for Kensal Green the Père-la-Chaise model was to be the basis upon which the design would be constructed. Within the general layout, as in Père-la-Chaise, the public was to be at liberty to erect whatever sort of monuments they pleased. The report on the new cemetery at Frankfurt was studied, and the design of the colonnades was eventually adopted from that example.

In September 1831 it was agreed that Mr Liddell should design the layout, after Sir John D. Paul had presented a sketch which had been 'drawn under the eye of Mr Nash'. Liddell had been at the Crown Office, under John Nash, who volunteered his assistance to the company. Liddell was experienced in major layouts; nevertheless, he withdrew his detailed plans in October, although the layout eventually adopted appears to be based on his scheme.

A report appeared in the *Gentleman's Magazine*[3] that on 24 July the shareholders of the General Cemetery Company held their first great meeting after their incorporation, at Exeter Hall, for the purpose of appointing directors, receiving a report from the 'provisional committee &c. Lord Ingestrie in the chair'. £9,400 had been laid out in the purchase of fifty-four acres at 'Kensall Green, on the Harrow Road'. A drainage scheme had been effected, and a boundary wall, to give privacy and protection to the property, was in the course of erection, and would probably be completed by the first of August. Entries nos 883 and 884 in vol 28 of the Westminster Sewer Plans show layouts of the cemetery signed by Mr Griffith in June 1832, 'to be deposited with the Honourable the Commissioners of Sewers', so progress must have been rapid. The committee reported that it had offered a reward of 100 guineas for the best designs for a chapel and entrance gates to the cemetery. A plantation of forest trees had been commenced, and 800 planted. The

The entrance to Kensal Green

subscribed capital was £36,725, of which £22,193 had been paid. Lord Ingestrie said, to conciliate the Bishop of London, that the clergy of the parish from which a body was taken were to be paid a fee of 5s for every body so removed, if interred in a vault, catacomb, or brick grave; and 1s 6d each if interred in the open ground; the rector of St Marylebone to receive an additional 2s 6d for each body, his salary being 'principally composed of burial fees'. At the same meeting Mr Bowman was elected clerk; Sir J. D. Paul, treasurer, and G. F. Carden, registrar. There appears to have been much delicacy of feeling over 'donating' money and actually possessing shares. Clearly certain persons felt that burial of the dead was no fit subject for speculation even at this early stage.

The notice of the architectural competition was noted in the minutes of 1 November 1831 (p76). The buildings required were to consist of a chapel with ample vaults. It

Kendall's design for the chapel at Kensal Green Cemetery. The lithograph was by Thomas Allom

was proposed that this building should be used for the sole purpose of performing the funeral service and for the advantageous display of monuments. The expense was not under any circumstances to exceed £10,000. Other requirements were for one Principal Entrance Gateway with a lodge or lodges, with accommodation of not less than four rooms, the expense of which was not to exceed £3,000. On 1 March 1832 the 100 guineas premium was awarded to H. E. Kendall of 17 Suffolk Street, Pall Mall, for his designs in the Gothic mode.[4]

Henry Edward Kendall died on 4 January 1875 at the ripe old age of ninety-eight, being born on 23 March 1776.[5] He was a pupil of Thomas Leverton, of Bedford Square fame, and of John Nash. He was a friend of Pugin, entering a design himself for the Houses of Parliament competition, and was a frequent exhibitor at the Royal Academy. His daughter married Lewis Cubitt. He went to the Barrack

Department of the War Office, and in 1823 became surveyor to the Districts of St Martin-in-the-Fields and that of St Anne, Soho. He was a founder of the Royal Institute of British Architects. In fact, he obtained both first premium for his Gothic design for Kensal Green and second premium for an Italian design, but he 'missed the building' as he 'refused to carry out the design of Sir John D. Paul, the Chairman of the Company, who completed and required his own design to be executed'![6]

On 19 March 1832 the committee of the General Cemetery Company resolved to accept Kendall's Gothic designs for building, but one member gave notice that he intended to press for the resolution to be rescinded. Kendall's 'Proposed Picturesque Arrangement' of the Cemetery Ground is remarkably fine, and includes winding avenues, a great circular avenue with a central monument, an extraordinary fantasy in Gothic for the chapel, a delightful water-gate through which funerals could proceed from the canal, and a

'Proposed Picturesque Arrangement of Cemetery Ground' by H. E. Kendall, for Kensal Green

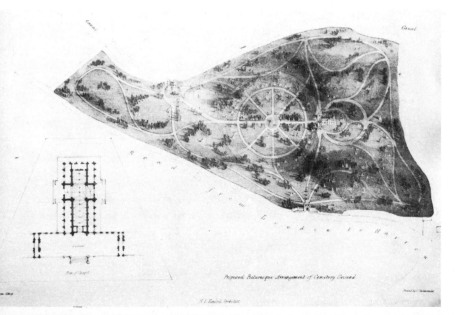

robust entrance gateway on the Harrow Road (pages 60, 61 and 63.) The *Gentleman's Magazine* of 1832[7] carries a review of Kendall's designs, and notes that a picturesque effect was sought; the pointed style being adopted as being that which harmonised best with the object for which the building was designed. 'The propriety of giving the preference to our own ecclesiastical architecture, on this occasion, will hardly be questioned, as it is associated in the minds of all, with ideas of devotion and religious feeling; it has a sanctity attached to it peculiarly suitable to a place designed to be the last home of mortality, which should be impressive and solemn.' 'When the Englishman wanders among the tombs of his forefathers; when his thoughts are fixed on the generations which have preceded him, he is little disposed at such a time

> With classic eye to trace
> Corinthian beauty or Ionic grace;

he cares not to have his attention called to other nations; he is then, in a peculiar sense, a denizen of the soil on which he stands, and his eye loves to dwell on such objects, and such only, as are in unison with the feelings of the moment.'

The elevation shows a nave and transept in rather a florid style of architecture, with which the critic could not agree. The slender proportions, as well as the number of Kendall's spires and pinnacles, seemed to the *Gentleman's Magazine* to be at variance with the 'sepulchral character' of the edifice, but the romantic lithographs by Thomas Allom which were published to illustrate Kendall's designs show very appropriate buildings for a cemetery. Of particular interest is the 'North East View of proposed Cemetery Chapel, Kensall Green' (page 60) which also shows a funeral procession approaching the chapel. The hearse is drawn by six black horses, and is topped by ostrich feathers. It is preceded by mutes with wands, and by feather-pages. This chapel was to

The Water Gate and main entrance to Kensal Green Cemetery, by H. E. Kendall. The lithograph is by Thomas Allom

be so placed that it could be seen from various parts of the ground, and was to be situated on a gentle slope about the centre of the cemetery which, on account of the 'elegant undulations of its surface', was thought capable by the aid of 'judicious planting, interspersed with tombs,' of being

[*63*]

made picturesque and beautiful. The chapel would contribute a 'chasteness at once appropriate and pleasing'.

The reviewer did not like the group of sculpture above the entrance gate, nor the inverted torches on the wings. The water-gate was to be in the same style of architecture as the chapel, but the critic recommended that, when it was erected, the word 'Cemetery' on the centre panel should be inscribed in a character 'corresponding with the age of the architecture, instead of Roman capitals . . .'. The review ends with general approval of the design of the cemetery, and contrasts it with those usual depositories of the dead, the churchyards and burying-grounds of the metropolis.

The minutes of the company for 1 March 1832[8] record that the author of design No 4 be requested to complete his drawings, and on 15 March Kendall was subjected to an inquisition on his scheme, some doubt being expressed about the suitability of the designs. In the ensuing squabbles Sir John Dean Paul, the chairman of the company, emerged victorious, so victorious that he has been credited with the design of the chapels. He was, in fact, only the banker who contributed sums of money, but he clearly imposed his will on the other members of the company.[9] His opposition to Kendall's design won the day, and Greek Revival was substituted for Gothic. As a result, G. F. Carden, who supported Kendall, was suspended in February 1833, and removed from the office of registrar in June. The designer of the cool Greek colonnades and Anglican chapel (page 65), together with the catacombs, the entrance gateway (page 59) and Noncomformist chapel appears to have been John William Griffith, the company's surveyor, and the minutes indicate that his plans for these were the ones accepted. However, the detailed drawings in the possession of the General Cemetery Company are signed by William Chadwick, who is known to have been described

The Anglican chapel designed by J. W. Griffith and William Chadwick at Kensal Green Cemetery. The tomb of Princess Sophia, designed by Gruner and executed by Signori Bardi of Carrara, and Messrs Noakes and Pearce of London, is on the right

as an architect, and was also active as a builder in the Kensington area. Since builders frequently doubled as architects at that time and often produced classical buildings based on readily available patterns, it seems safe to assume that the clear and precise drawings signed by Chadwick indicate that he was responsible for the details of the individual buildings at Kensal Green, although Griffith drew up Sir John Dean Paul's requirements in broad outline beforehand. The surveyor is certain to have drawn up the site plans and drainage diagrams, and indeed the minutes for 20 September 1831 (p 68) confirm this, for Griffith was instructed to furnish plans and sections of the ground to lay before the committee. Griffith also drew up the working plans for enclosing the ground on the north side of the canal, and it was he, in his capacity as surveyor, who had overall responsibility for building and layout works which were largely implementations of Liddell's earlier designs. Griffith's signature appears on the plans deposited with the Commissioners of Sewers in 1832. Described as 'An Architect of Finsbury' in the minutes, he was surveyor of St Botolph, Aldersgate, and to the London Estates of St John's College, Cambridge. He designed many villas in London, and also the Islington Parochial Schools. A Mr Griffith was chairman of the General Cemetery Company between 1864 and 1880, but, according to Colvin, the architect died in 1855.

Both the chapels at Kensal Green are prostyle tetrastyle, the Anglican being Doric (page 65), while the Nonconformist chapel is Ionic. Both have brick vaulted catacombs underneath, Piranesian in intensity, with stone coffin racks and cast-iron protective grilles of similar detail to typical domestic balconies of the period. The gateway, which includes the lodges and offices, is on the Harrow Road, and has a bold Doric treatment over a triumphal arch. The quality of conception and design is excellent, and Chadwick seems to have had a sure and confident touch.

On 25 November 1831 it was resolved that 'Mr Pugin and Mr Griffith should meet Mr Forrest at Sir John D. Paul's at one o'clock on Saturday' to proceed to the ground for the purpose of making a plan for the partial planting of the ground, 'Mr Forrest's plan produced not being approved of, and that Sir J. D. Paul be authorised to give directions for such planting in pursuance of the resolution at the last meeting to that effect'. By 12 December 1831 Griffith could report that it was agreed that the plantation should be carried out round the cemetery, and that this was being done. It is minuted for the same day that there had been a proposal for laying out the ground from Mr David Ramsay of the Stanhope Nursery, Old Brompton, but this proposal was turned down. Ramsay's work is significant at Highgate and Brompton Cemeteries and will be discussed later in this book. Three days later the committee agreed to ask Sir John Soane for testimonials concerning Chadwick, who had carried out numerous contracts under the great Soane's direction.

The *Gentleman's Magazine*[10] reported that the Bishop of London consecrated the burial-ground of the 'General Cemetery Company, at Kensall Green'.[11] The whole thirty-nine acres to the north of the Regent's Canal, which had been enclosed within a lofty wall, were consecrated; and the space of 'fifteen acres on the other side of the Canal' was reserved for Dissenters, whose services could not be performed on ground attached to the Established Church. A temporary chapel had been erected, the design for the permanent edifice not being determined upon. The first interment was made on 31 January, of the corpse of 'Margaret, wife of Bernard Gregory, esq. of Great Russell-street to whose memory the Directors of the Company intend, from gratitude to their first customer, to erect a tablet at their own expense. Several other interments have since taken place.' The subdivision by the canal is clearly a mistake, for the Paddington Canal bounded the south side of the site. The only subdivision was a right of way which is shown on one of the maps deposited with the Honourable the Commissioners of Sewers. The consecration of the Cemetery of All Souls, Kensal Green, was reported in *The Times*, the date of consecration being November 1832, but the minutes of the company state that consecration took place on 24 January 1833, and the latter date appears to be the correct one.

The materials chosen for the buildings were Portland stone and Roman cement. The cemetery was remarkably advanced for its time, being divided into areas 150ft by 100ft, thus ensuring an accurate system of mapping into plots.[12] Each plot could be bought as a freehold, and this freehold could be bequeathed by the owner. Each plot was annotated in massive, bound ledgers. No coffin could be nearer than 4ft from the surface, so the worst aspects of the churchyards were provided with an antidote in All Souls. A most interesting innovation was the inclusion of a hydraulic lowering device in the chapel so that coffins could be brought down into the catacombs beneath at the end of the service. This bronze catafalque still exists, and shows that modern crematorium catafalques have hardly improved in either design or function.

Walford, in *Old and New London*,[13] wrote that no sooner was the cemetery opened than the boon was eagerly embraced by the public, and 'marble obelisks and urns began to rise among the cypresses in all the variety which heathen and classical allusions could suggest'. Against the northern boundary wall, and parallel with the Episcopal chapel, is a small colonnade, and beneath this are the old or original catacombs. Every space in these vaults was quickly occupied, and the extensive colonnades and chambers for the erection of tablets to the memory of persons whose remains are laid in the catacombs below are 'spots where the visitor to the cemetery may find an almost endless number of subjects for meditation'.

Certainly the catacombs under the Anglican chapel are awesome. In the dark vaults thousands of coffins, once clothed in rich-hued velvets secured to the wood by brass studs, lie in serried rows. There is a large number of children's coffins. Some of the wood has rotted; and the lead lining may be seen. Today the catacombs are an

Catacombs beneath the Anglican Chapel at Kensal Green Cemetery

extraordinary reminder of the heroic age of cemetery design.

Immediately before the Anglican chapel are several tombs of excellent design, among them the beautiful quattrocento sarcophagus, designed by Gruner and made by the Signori Bardi, that stands on a mighty podium executed by Edward Pearce, and marks the burial place of Princess

Sophia, daughter of George III, who died in 1848 (page 65). Near by is the huge slab which covers the remains of the Duke of Sussex, the brother of the princess. The duke, who died in 1843, was so shocked by the delay and confusion at the funeral of King William IV that he declared he would not be buried at Windsor. The famous Duke of Cambridge also lies in Kensal Green, Queen Victoria having purchased sites for royal mausolea in 1849.

Other celebrities are buried in this huge cemetery, where the trees are now mature, and the profusion of rich monuments, many of them sadly neglected and smashed by vandals, speak eloquently of a wide range of changing tastes. Thackeray, Trollope, Brunel, Millais, Browning, Leigh Hunt, Feargus O'Connor, Mulready, Cruickshank, John Sievier, John Murray, and Sir Robert Smirke are among many distinguished people buried in the cemetery of All Souls, adjacent to which is the Roman Catholic cemetery of St Mary, designed by S. J. Nicholl of 126 Marylebone Road, and consecrated on 11 June 1859. Cardinal Wiseman was interred here, as was Manning, before their translation to Westminster Cathedral. But St Mary's is full of undistinguished tomb and monument designs. It is a relief to return to the General Cemetery and to find tombs of quality such as that of the Molyneux family, by John Gibson, of 1866, in the most florid Victorian Gothic (page 71); that to Sir John Long by Sievier; and the Ward monument by Foley.

Not long after it had been established, Kensal Green became one of the sights of London. The *Mirror of Literature, Amusement and Instruction*[14] published a view of the General Cemetery, Kensal Green together with an account of the costs of burial. A single interment in the catacombs cost six guineas, and a purchased grave, with privilege of placing a monument, flat, or head and foot stones cost five guineas. A single interment in a grave, inclusive of all ordinary fees, was priced at twenty-five shillings, while ground for a vault or brick grave cost fifteen guineas. The *Mirror* declared that 'the contiguity of a burial-ground and railway is calculated to sadden the casual visitor: upon one occasion, at the close of a delightful day of repose, we remember to have stood in a charming meadow hard by, and there to have contrasted the clear yet chilling note of the

Gibson's mausoleum to the Molyneux family at Kensal Green. The spire has since been demolished

THE GENERAL CEMETERY, KENSAL GREEN.

General view of Kensal Green Cemetery. Ducrow's mausoleum is in the foreground. The Anglican chapel is in the background. From The Mirror of Literature, Amusement, and Instruction, *no 890, 28 April 1838*

Cemetery chapel bell with the almost indescribable noise of the approaching engine and its train upon the railway many yards beneath. The position was of painful interest; and we turned from thence to the all-glorious sun, then tinging the western horizon with a flood of crimson light, and in its splendour reminding us how puny are the proudest triumphs of Art in comparison with the majesty of Nature.'

Despite the somewhat flowery description, it is clear from the minutes that there was much consternation in case the railway would drive through the company's land. Griffith had already met Stephenson, the surveyor of the London & Birmingham Railway Company, to see what effect the new line would have on the General Cemetery Company's land.

[72]

The committee thought that the railway would be prejudicial in the highest degree to the new cemetery. It was resolved on 19 March 1832 that the Birmingham Railroad Company should pay an adequate compensation for the land forming the site of the tunnel and the damages which the Cemetery Company would suffer from 'forming the same'. Problems arose to the south also, for there the Grand Junction Canal was seeking land. Involved in the negotiations was C. Pleydell Bouverie, later the chairman of Brompton Cemetery, who agreed with Sir J. D. Paul that £1,200 should be paid to the canal company to help form an embankment which would mean that less land would be lost to the cemetery. These negotiations were broken off in consequence of the report that a footpath existed through the land on the opposite side of the canal. Mr Griffith was duly instructed to proceed with the building of brick walls and iron railings.

Griffith agreed to be remunerated with whatever compensation the committee might award. At a meeting on 12 July 1832 Sir J. D. Paul produced plans and estimates for catacombs by a Mr Moseley, the consideration of which was deferred. It is obvious that Paul held the committee in the palm of his hand, and Griffith was clearly told what to do, taking aspects of various designs suggested by Paul. It is here that the confusion has arisen over the authorship of the chapels.

The *Mirror*[15] was of the opinion that in the future surveys of London, the cemetery at Kensal Green must hold a distinguished place, not only for itself but for its 'numerous progeny'. This was the first 'establishment of its kind, of any magnitude, in or near the capital of the British empire'. Obviously, the *Mirror*, like most opinion at the time, thoroughly approved of the new cemetery, comparing it with the state of affairs where year after year funerals had continued to be performed in the churchyards, though it had been well ascertained that to inter one body it was necessary to eject another. 'To the evil those under whose observation it was necessarily brought continued resolutely to shut their eyes.'

Even now, despite many hideous modern monuments; despite the overgrown state of much of the grounds; despite the decay of the Dissenters' chapel, now in a ruinous state, and of the catacombs by the wall on the Harrow Road, Kensal Green Cemetery has a grandeur which is deeply moving. Not only is the main chapel an extremely distinguished essay in Greek Revival (page 65), but all the other buildings also are of considerable interest. The main chapel is undistinguished inside, and the hydraulic lift mechanism no longer functions, but the catacombs underneath are very impressive. Unfortunately the chapel and arcades were hit by bombs on 27 September 1940. They were partially restored in 1954 under the direction of E. R. Bingham Harriss, but much of the original conception was lost. One wonders if it was in fact the chapels or the gate lodge which was damaged in an earlier fire, for records exist concerning a turncock belonging to the West Middlesex Waterworks Company, 'whose water came first into the Main where a Plug was opened at a Fire' which happened on 18 August 1865 at the premises belonging to 'the Cemitary [*sic*] situate at Kensal Green . . .'. The fire was put out by no fewer than three engines, and we learn that the said 'Turncock did turn on the Water and draw a Plug at the said Fire, as aforesaid; and that the said Engine Keepers did bring the said Engines in good order and complete with Socket, Hose and Leather Pipe, to the said Fire'.[16]

The Dissenters' chapel is now used as a lumber room, and is rather an embarrassment to the company, who wish to demolish it. A Preservation Order has prevented this, but unfortunately there appear to be no funds available to restore this rather charming little Ionic temple. The General Cemetery Company still pays dividends, and use of monies to restore a building no longer needed would no doubt be unsound policy.

Breaking into mausolea and smashing up coffins appears to be a current trend, so many of the robustly built tombs have suffered. The whole range of Victorian taste is displayed in this cemetery, from chaste classical tombstones to wild Gothic fantasies, like Gibson's high Victorian Gothic Octagon (page 71). Ducrow's Egyptian-style mausoleum of 1837 looks as though it could have been by Geary, who published books of designs which are incredibly coarse,[17] but Ducrow's tomb was, in fact, by Dawson. *The Builder*[18] denounced the taste of the monuments in Kensal Green, Ducrow's tomb being described as an example of 'ponderous coxcombry', but the monument to Hood, designed by Noble, was praised in another issue.[19] The inscription on Ducrow's tomb declares that 'Within this tomb erected by genius for the reception of its own remains are deposited those of Andrew Ducrow, many years lessee of the Royal Amphitheatre, London, whose death deprived the arts and sciences of an eminent professor and liberal patron' (page 72). Ducrow had buried his wife in 1835, and the funeral was recorded by an 'Old Stager' who had known the showman. The site for the tomb cost one hundred pounds, and the construction of the vault cost forty more, the space to be made ready in five days. When the day of the interment came, however, it was found that the vault had 3ft of water in it, and the ground all around was a deep puddle of clay and water. There was a terrible scene in the chapel when Ducrow called the clergyman who was officiating a 'swindling old humbug' for taking one hundred and fifty pounds from him and then not having the vault ready. He said he would take his wife's body home again, but his friends advised him to leave it in the chapel, and this he did, taking the company's keys with him. Ducrow then tried to have his wife buried in St Paul's or Westminster Abbey, but eventually agreed to have the coffin placed in the catacombs at Kensal Green until the celebrated Egyptian Mausoleum could be made ready the following August, when the body was removed from the catacombs to the new tomb. Dawson's design cost £3,000 to build, and Ducrow left the sum of £500, the interest of which was to keep the mausoleum in good repair, including the ground and railing. It is a matter of speculation what has become of this money, for the tomb is not in 'good repair' any more, and the ground is overgrown. Most of the railing has disappeared.

E. W. Trendall also published a book of designs,[20] as did J. B. Bunning.[21] Knight comments in his *London* on the style and quality of tomb design. 'Largeness of Structure' is not to be thought of as being synonymous with grandeur, and a really good idea tends to suffer from endless repetitions. 'The stately Corinthian column, broken midway in its height, is a noble type of man cut down in his prime; but what if, instead of imitating the work, the artists of the cemetery would imitate him who designed it, that is, think for themselves?' Indeed, it is fascinating to study contemporary accounts of the funerary architecture. The opinion of most of the monuments was very low, but J. H. Foley's monument to James Ward (engraver and painter) is mentioned in *The Builder* of 7 November 1863, and Edward Blore's design[22] for the tomb of General Forster Walker is praised in the issue dated 8 April 1866. Many tombs were by E. M. Lander, of Kensal Green.

Kensal Green is a melancholy place in winter, but in the summer the leafiness of the landscaped walks contrasts admirably with the wealth of sculptural monuments and

Kensal Green. 'The leafiness of the landscaped walks contrasts admirably with the wealth of sculptural monuments and with the rich architecture of the mausolea.'

with the rich architecture of the mausolea (above). Yet an air of decay hastened by vandalism can cease to be pleasing, and it is clear that labour costs and indifference will contribute to the erosion of the splendid monument of early cemetery design.[23]

4 The architecturally distinguished private enterprise cemeteries established after Kensal Green

Underneath this stone doth lie
As much beauty as could die;
Which in life did harbour give
To more virtue than doth live.
If at all she had a fault,
Leave it buried in this vault.

Ben Jonson

The South Metropolitan Cemetery at Norwood

By 1839 Kensal Green cemetery was described as being a flourishing concern, and the original £25 shares of the General Cemetery Company were priced at £52.[1] Such success encouraged the formation of other cemeteries, which followed in rapid succession from 1837. The first of these later private cemeteries was established at Norwood by the South Metropolitan Cemetery Company. It comprised some forty acres; and was consecrated by the Bishop of Winchester on 6 December 1837.[2]

The architect to the company was none other than the celebrated Sir William Tite, who numbers the Royal Exchange among his works. Tite was born on 7 February 1798 in the parish of St Bartholomew the Great, Smithfield. He was a pupil of David Laing and obtained most of his early experience designing railway termini. He became an FSA in 1839 and was vice-president in 1860. He planned Brookwood Cemetery near Woking in 1853-4. He became president of the RIBA in 1861-3 and again from 1867 to 70; and was knighted in 1869. He died in Torquay in 1873 on 20 April and was buried in the vaults at Norwood Cemetery on 26 April.

Tite's design was fine and spacious, with an English landscape of clumps of trees and wide open spacious lawns leading to the chapels up the hill. These chapels, one for Anglicans, and the other for Dissenters, were in Perpendicular Gothic, constructed of stock bricks with Portland stone dressings. There were Gothic arcaded wings, with catacombs underneath. Unfortunately, the chapels were badly damaged in World War II, and they have been replaced by a crematorium of uninspired design. A print of the 1840s shows Norwood as originally laid out and demonstrates that it was a very splendid conception. It is of particular interest to compare Tite's design with J. C.

Sir William Tite's plan for Norwood Cemetery

Loudon's proposals, here illustrated. In the foreground may be seen a funeral procession approaching the gates of the cemetery, preceded by mutes with crape-swathed wands and a feather-page carrying ostrich feathers. The horses have black ostrich-feather plumes, and their saddles are draped with black. Of some interest is the hearse which is of the old box type with closed sides and no ornament, the more exuberantly Baroque varieties only coming into fashion in the 1870s. These old prints give some idea of the spaciousness which the Victorians sought to give their cemeteries, and of the surprisingly rural setting of the South Metropolitan Cemetery. Today, with the whole area almost a solid mass of surburban housing, and with the cemetery an equally solid mass of tombstones, the nobility of Tite's design has been sorely eroded.

John Claudius Loudon is one of those towering nineteenth-century figures; a self-made man *par excellence*. From humble beginnings he rose to a position of eminence as editor of the *Gardener's Magazine* and as a prolific writer on architecture and landscaping. Loudon wrote a book *On the laying out, planting and managing of Cemeteries: and on the improvement of Churchyards, with sixty engravings,* which was published as one volume in London in 1843. It had originally appeared as a series of articles in the *Gardener's Magazine,* but was reprinted as a book later, and is crammed with information on all sorts of details connected with cemeteries. Loudon advised hermetically sealed coffins in vaults or catacombs, and warned of the poor practices of managing family graves in that there was not sufficient earth between coffins, six feet of earth over every coffin being his standard.

Loudon defined the uses of a cemetery to include the disposal of the remains of the dead in such a manner as that their decomposition, and return to the earth from which

J. C. Loudon's proposals for Norwood Cemetery

they sprang, should not prove injurious to the living either by affecting their health, or 'shocking their feelings, opinions, or prejudices. A *secondary object* is, or ought to be, the improvement of the moral sentiments and general taste of all classes, and more especially of the great masses of society.' He advised that the building of sepulchres would soon have to be discontinued. A coffin having been buried, he wrote, should never be disturbed, and he quoted Jewish cemeteries as examples of excellence in this respect.[3]

On page four he recalled the several unpleasant incidents when coffins in the vaults of the new London cemeteries had exploded, and undertakers were sent for in order to re-solder the lead coffins to contain the corruption. Scientists and medical men of the day were puzzled about the exact composition of the gases produced by a decomposing body, and experiments with lighted candles were carried out when a lead coffin did in fact leak.[4] He rightly pointed out the difficulties in London posed by the heavy clay which did not allow gases to escape, for there was always the problem that, when a grave-digger was working to reopen a grave, he could break through the coffin lid with disastrous results, and Loudon noted with disapproval that gravediggers were frequently plied with rum to render their sensibilities less active. Loudon sensibly suggested that a layer of slate or tile should be laid six feet over the last coffin to avoid mishaps and show the exact point where the next coffin could lie.

In order to prevent the graves being rifled, despite the fact that the resurrectionists were not as active after the passing of the Poor Law Amendment Act of 1844, Loudon suggested that an iron box should be let down over the grave, to be drawn up by machinery after eight weeks, when the body would be too far decomposed to be of use to the resurrection men. Another method suggested by

Loudon of establishing whether a grave had in fact been rifled was to plant flowers on top, which, if disturbed, would show signs of wilting.

There is much detail of this kind in Loudon's book, but its chief interest is in his advice on planting and his comments on the contemporary cemeteries.[5] The *Coemeterion* of the Greek suggested only the idea of a bed of slumber, while the cemetery of the Jew in the Bible spoke 'but of the mansion of the living'. A general cemetery, properly laid out, ornamented with tombs, planted with trees, shrubs, and herbaceous plants, all named, and the whole properly kept, 'might become a school of instruction in architecture, sculpture, landscape gardening, arboriculture, botany, and in those important parts of general gardening, neatness, order, and high keeping'. Abney Park Cemetery was quoted, having a grand entrance in Egyptian architecture, 'a handsome Gothic chapel . . . and one of the most complete arboretums in the neighbourhood of London, all the trees and shrubs being named'.[6]

Loudon summed up his attitude to cemeteries with the statement that 'Churchyards and cemeteries are scenes not only calculated to improve the morals and the taste, and by their botanical riches to cultivate the intellect, but they serve as *historical records*'. *The Builder*[7] thought this sentence was so important that it quoted it in full. The tomb has, in fact, been the 'great chronicler of taste' throughout the world. With regard to the layout, Loudon advised the selection of ground with a southern aspect, dry, or capable of being drained, not connected with drinking-water, and convenient to centres of population. He praised the combination of gateway and lodge, as in the West of London and Westminster Cemetery and Kensal Green, although he thought Wyatt and Brandon's lodge at Tower Hamlets Cemetery was the best designed. He criticised

Norwood for having two chapels placed equally near the eye, in the same plane, and so far apart as not to group together. He was highly critical of Tite's landscaping, and suggested a scheme of his own superimposed on Tite's layout (pages 80 and 81). He recommended *Pinus Taurica*, *Pinus Pallasiana*, or *Pinus Nigranus* for the main avenue, while along the walks he advised the planting of Irish yews, Swedish junipers, box, and other similar plants. Ash or weeping willows were useful trees to punctuate a vista or to provide focal points.

Loudon was very interested in the chapel mechanism in Kensal Green, and described it. The machine could turn the bier round, or if interment was to take place in the catacombs, the bier was slowly lowered through the floor, and mourners could then descend into the vaults, which covered one acre. The machine was invented by Mr Smith, engineer, of Princes Street, Leicester Square. In Norwood the same object was achieved with Bramah's hydraulic press, made by Bramah, Prestage & Ball, of 124 Piccadilly.

When the South Metropolitan Cemetery Company established Norwood Cemetery in 1837,[8] it did so under legislation;[9] for Kensal Green had set the precedent for the setting up of Joint Stock Companies to operate cemeteries. The South Metropolitan Cemetery Company was empowered to open a cemetery of up to eighty acres, within ten miles of London, to build two chapels, and to raise capital up to £75,000. The land bought consisted of forty-one acres of copyhold land in Lambeth Manor which had once belonged to Lord Thurlow, and which had been surrendered by his trustees. The land was immediately enfranchised by the company, and the wall was constructed shortly afterwards.

Apart from the boundary wall and railings and the basic layout and planting, little remains of Sir William Tite's conception. Surviving prints showing the prospect of the cemetery in the 1840s give us an excellent idea of its romantic qualities before it was covered with marble and the peaceful rural charm was lost. However, the cemetery is of particular interest to us today for the extraordinary number of excellent Victorian monuments still standing. Also of interest is the Greek Cemetery, which lies within the north-eastern corner of the main cemetery.

In 1842 this land was acquired by the Brotherhood of the Greek Community in London. In 1872 another piece of land was added, and in the same year Stephen Ralli obtained permission to erect a small chapel in memory of his son. This was designed by John Oldrid Scott, and is Greek Doric, with tetrastyle portico. Near the chapel is a mausoleum, also for the Ralli family, by the celebrated G. E. Street.

In 1847 the parish of St Mary-at-Hill, in the City, acquired a small piece of land in the south-east corner of the cemetery, an interesting innovation for the times. In 1892 several bodies were removed from the crypt of St Mary-at-Hill, and re-interred in Norwood.

Among famous people buried at Norwood, Jeremiah Colman, Sir Henry Tate, Sir Henry Doulton, Sir Henry Bessemer, Sir William Cubitt, David Cox, Samuel Prout, and Mrs Beeton should be mentioned.[10]

In 1966 Norwood was acquired by Lambeth Borough Council, whose architect, Mr Hollamby, was anxious to record as much as possible of the existing cemetery. In a report by Nicholas Taylor for the Victorian Society, the fact that the South Metropolitan Cemetery had become overcrowded with resulting difficulties of upkeep and unarrested decay was emphasised. Mr Taylor demonstrated that it was almost impossible to see the cemetery as a whole, but that it might still be possible to remodel it to restore its original beauties of landscape and sculpture, while at the same time making it possible for the Borough's cemetery superintendent to maintain it 'economically with a small staff . . . If it is essential for the Borough to remodel the whole Cemetery comprehensively it is also essential for a comprehensive scheme of conservation to be worked out which will ensure the repair and maintenance in the best possible condition of the best monuments . . .' Mr Taylor recommended clearance of undergrowth so that a proper survey could be carried out. I agree entirely with him that the cemetery is a 'major monument of national importance of the landscape design of the early 19th century'. It is a major tragedy that Tite's scheme cannot be restored, and it is shameful that the Anglican chapel was demolished as late as 1960.[11]

Many distinguished architects besides Tite and Street are represented in Norwood Cemetery. Thomas Allom's mausoleum for George Dodd in florid Gothic is a case in point; while E. M. Barry's monument to the Berens family is an example of that florid mid-Victorian style so symbolic of worldly success. E. M. Barry and T. H. Vernon designed yet another Ralli mausoleum, this time for Eustratios Ralli, which can be found in the Greek Cemetery.[12]

Highgate Cemetery

Highgate Cemetery must have first claim to being the most unashamedly romantic of all the cemeteries in Britain. Like many others of the period, it was founded by a Joint Stock Company, and the costliness of interment as a result hardly abated the problems of intramural burial, especially for the mass of the populace.

The Cemetery of St James at Highgate was established by the London Cemetery Company, which had offices at 29 New Bridge Street, London, EC. It is situated on either side of Swain's Lane, and the older part to the west at one time formed part of the grounds of the mansion belonging to Sir William Ashurst. The company, like the General Cemetery Company and the South Metropolitan Cemetery Company, was formed to promote the improvements so badly needed to cater for the interment of the dead of a great metropolis. The founder of the firm was Stephen Geary, who also acted as architect to the company, which was incorporated in 1836. It is in connection with Highgate Cemetery that we first come across Geary, an extraordinary *entrepreneur* and architect who specialised in cemetery design. Stephen Geary, architect and civil engineer, practised at Hamilton Place, New Road, London. He is remembered primarily for his design of an octagonal structure with a colossal statue of George IV on the top, erected in the centre of the space where six roads merged at Battle Bridge when the name was changed to King's Cross in 1831. He was an inventor, taking out patents for artificial fuel; for paving streets; for water supply; for obtaining motive power: and for three other patented inventions between 1838 and 1843. He is credited with the design of the first gin palace in London, circa 1830. He founded the London Cemetery Company in 1838, for which he laid out Highgate Cemetery, opened 20 May 1839. He died at 19 Euston Place, London, on 28 August 1854, aged 74.[13] His tombstone in Highgate Cemetery read:

Sacred
to the Memory of
STEPHEN GEARY, Esqre.,
Architect and Founder of this Cemetery,
who departed this life Augt 28th, 1854,
in the 75th year of his age.
Also of SARAH, widow of the above,
who died on the 19th of July, 1867,
aged 69 years.[14]

Today, however, there is no sign of his monument, which was placed obscurely in the fourth rank in from 'Road B'.

A portion of the cemetery was consecrated on 20 May 1839 by the Bishop of London. The Rev Dr Russell was the chairman. This original consecration was of some twenty-two acres, but a portion was left unconsecrated for the interment of Dissenters.

The 'Act for establishing Cemeteries for the Interment of the Dead, Northward, Southward and Eastward of the Metropolis by a Company to be called "The London Cemetery Company"' was dated 17 August 1836 (6 and 7 William IV, c 136, local). The Act incorporated the proprietors in a company. It stated that three cemeteries were to be established: in Surrey, in Kent, and in Middlesex, for the Parishes of Camberwell, St Pancras, St Matthew Bethnal Green, Whitechapel, Stepney, Bow, Mile End, Stratford, Bethnal Green, and Hackney. The company was empowered to lay out and to embellish the same in and with such 'Paths, Walks, Avenues, Roads, Trees, Shrubs, and Plantations as may be fitting and proper, and to cause such Cemeteries or Burial Grounds respectively to be inclosed with proper and sufficient Walls, Rails, Fences, Palisades, Gates, and Entrances, and any other Protections which may be thought necessary'. The Act contained a special section dealing with the prevention of contamination of private springs or wells. Part of the cemetery was to be for the Established Church, and part for the interment of Dissenters. The company was further empowered to build chapels for burial services, according to the rites of Dissenters and of the Established Church; and to build catacombs. No chapel with bells was to be built within 300 yards of the south boundary wall of the 'present District Church of *Highgate* in the Parish of *Saint Pancras* in the County of *Middlesex*'.

[*88*]

The company was empowered to sell exclusive rights of burial in vaults in perpetuity or for a limited period. In any case the purchasers were required immediately upon the completion of 'such Purchase, to close the Entrance of each such Catacomb, Vault, or Place of Burial with good and substantial Doors to the satisfaction of the said Company, under the Penalty of Five Pounds'.

Of great interest today, in view of the state of Highgate and Nunhead, is the clause which read: 'The said Company shall, by and out of the monies to be received by virtue of this Act, keep the said Cemeteries respectively and the said Chapel or Chapels respectively, and the several Buildings thereon and therein, and the external Walls and Fences thereof, and all other Parts of the same, in thorough and complete Repair.' A full plan was to be kept by the clerk.

The company was to pay a fee on the interment of persons removed from certain parishes, and was to 'keep Account of such Fees and allow an Inspection thereof'. Provision was made for penalties to be imposed on persons injuring the cemeteries or committing nuisances. Furthermore, 'it shall not be lawful for the said Company, under the Authority of the Provisions herein-before contained, to sell or dispose of any land which shall have been consecrated, or set apart or used for the Burial of the Dead'.

Both sides of the cemetery total some fifty acres, and Lloyd described it as the most picturesque cemetery of the north of London.[15] The original part of the cemetery, covering some twenty acres on the southern slope of the hill (obeying Loudon's dictum), was landscaped by David Ramsay, the company's landscape gardener, whose ingenious treatment of the planting of winding, circuitous roads with footpaths making off in all directions is responsible for the surprisingly spacious feel of the grounds (page 90).[16]

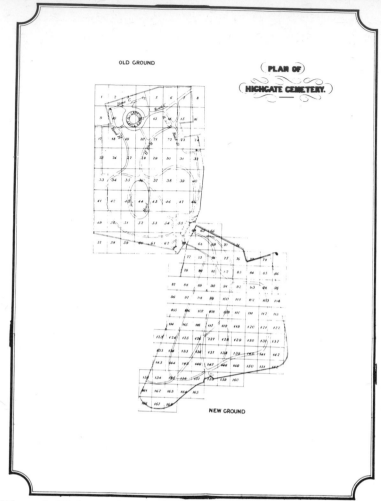

Plan of Highgate Cemetery (from Justyne's Guide to Highgate Cemetery)

On top of the hill is St Michael's Church, which has a fine spire and appears to be an integral part of the cemetery design. The church, ordered by the Church Commissioners, was designed by Lewis Vulliamy, built by Cubitt, and consecrated by the Bishop of London on 8 November 1832.[17]

Frederick Prickett describes the cemetery as possessing

[*90*]

a chapel for the use of members of the Established Church and of Dissenters on making interments, extensive ranges of catacombs, and a variety of tombs and vaults. The subterranean depositories and the beautifully diversified grounds were in 1842 improved under the 'judicious management of Mr J. B. Bunning, the architect of the company; and the whole forms a pleasing and ornamental addition to the hamlet'.[18] The 'neatly constructed Chapel', described by Lloyd as 'Undertakers' Gothic'[19] is very pretty indeed, and combines with entrance gates and lodge in a charming composition. The chapel has octagonal buttresses and bay windows, and possessed mechanically sophisticated devices for lowering coffins so that they could be taken out by a different route—a development of the Kensal Green idea. Timbs describes the cemetery as having a Tudor gate-house and chapel, and catacombs of Egyptian architecture; the ground is laid out in terraces, tastefully planted; and the distant view of the overgrown metropolis, from among the tombs, 'is suggestive to a meditative mind'.[20]

Lloyd noted that on entering the ground the eye is struck by the taste with which nature is combined with art, all the beauties of situations being improved by cultivation and 'taken the finest advantage of'. A contemporary newspaper in 1839 said of Highgate Cemetery that the undertaking seemed eminently successful, and excited some envy among its competitors. Many people had doubtless looked upon Paris from the tomb-clad hills of Père-la-Chaise, but from Highgate cemetery they could behold a vaster and more widely spreading scene, which Europe could not equal. The spectator might vainly try to grasp the extent of the 'modern Babylon', and left the sacred spot with the feeling that he was the citizen of a great country and in a metropolis worthy of its grandeur.

The first burial in St James's Cemetery was that of the body of Mrs Elizabeth Jackson of Little Windmill Street, Golden Square. Her tombstone still exists. The *Guide to Highgate Cemetery*[21] takes us first to the chapel, which adjoins the entrance, and was admirably fitted for its solemn purpose. 'The interior of the sacred edifice is spacious and lofty ... A bier, which can be gradually lowered through an opening in the floor by hydraulic pressure, stands at the western extremity'. The object of this bier was to convey the coffin to the subterranean passage below at the termination of the desk service, and so to facilitate its conveyance to the new ground on the other side of the lane. 'If nothing else gave evidence of the mournful purpose of the building, this alone would tell the sad story'. The Dissenters' chapel was to the right of the entrance gate, while the Anglican one was to the left. The chapels are in a lamentable state today, for they have lost all their pinnacles, and the vaulting has been removed. Filled with lumber, old burial registers, and rubbish, they clearly pronounce the ephemeral nature of the Victorian ideal.

There are other enthusiastic accounts in *The Mirror of Literature, Amusement and Instruction*,[22] and in *The Literary World*.[23] Some *Lines, occasioned by a visit to the Kentish-town and Highgate Cemetery, in company with my wife*, in an unidentified paper, possibly the *Penny Magazine of the Society for the Diffusion of Useful Knowledge*, are worth quoting, to demonstrate the extraordinary impact the early cemeteries had on contemporary imaginations:

> The day was fair, but not too bright,
> When through the meadows, rich in green,
> We took our way, and kept in sight
> The church that topt the upland scene.
> The very light the heav'ns threw out
> Seem'd shrouded with a velvet pall,

The trees and hedge-rows round about,
The hills, and dales, the skies and all
The various objects far and near
Appear'd, involv'd in light and shade;
And yet 'twas all obscurely-clear,
As if the Deity had made
The picture for the contemplation
Of adoration's musing eye,
And solemniz'd the situation,
Where I should wish our bones to lie.

*'An archway of the "stern and appropriate architecture of Egypt" leads
into the Egyptian Avenue.' The catacombs at Highgate*

Perhaps the most astonishing feature of the cemetery, however, is the series of buildings which form the catacombs. An archway of the 'stern and appropriate architecture of Egypt'[24] leads into the Egyptian Avenue and up a slope to the Circle of Lebanon catacombs, which are surmounted by a splendid cedar. These catacombs would make an ideal stage set for Mozart's *Die Zauberflöte*, especially for the Temple of Isis and Osiris scenes. The Egyptian Avenue has entrances to tombs on either side as it ascends the hill, and the lowering of the flanking walls with the ascent contributes to the illusion of great length (page 95). Each tomb is a square compartment with stone shelves for the coffins, and access to each compartment is through sadly decayed cast-iron doors. The entrances to each unit display a curious mixture of Egyptian and Greek Revival (page 93). Around the Lebanon Circle are yet more sepulchres (page 96). The inner circle thus formed has tombs round its circumference, while from the centre, on the higher level, grows the tree itself. Steps lead up from this circular street of tombs to the higher ground dominated by the enormous mausoleum of Julius Beer and by St Michael's Church. At this level there is a long range of catacombs in the Gothic taste, with buttresses, and from here there is a wonderful view of the London skyline. Many of the chambers, however, have been broken into recently (1970), and coffins have been ripped open to expose their grim contents. Such obscene vandalism is hard to understand, but appears to be a symptom of the times.

It is clear from an examination of the contemporary material that the Cedar of Lebanon Circle was completed first. An engraving[25] shows the cedar growing out from the centre of a circular series of tombs built under the ground, with sloping soil all round forming a variety of ditch. That Geary designed this there can be no doubt, but the circle of

The Egyptian Avenue in Highgate Cemetery

catacombs which formed the other side of the 'street' around the original circle may not have been by him. These were called the New Catacombs and appear to have been constructed shortly after the Egyptian Avenue. Somewhere between 1839 and 1842 much of the layout was designed by J. B. Bunning, who seems to have taken over the practical side of things from Geary, who was involved in the formation of several cemeteries at the time. The Gothic catacomb range at the highest point of the terrace is undoubtedly by Bunning.

The 'New Catacombs' at Highgate on the left. The original Lebanon Circle catacombs are on the right. The new catacombs were probably by J. B. Bunning

James Bunstone Bunning was born in London on 6 October 1802. He is described as an 'Architect in London, Surveyor of the Foundling Hospital Estates, 1825'.[26] He worked for his father and also for George Smith. He submitted a design for the Houses of Parliament Competition, as did H. E. Kendall who won the competition for the best designs for Kensal Green Cemetery. Bunning built the City of London School which was opened on 2 February 1837. He was appointed surveyor to the London Cemetery Company in 1839, and appears to have relieved Geary of much of the practical work, although Highgate had already been designed in broad outline by its founder. Bunning, however, laid out Nunhead Cemetery, also owned by the London Cemetery Company, the chapels being designed by Thomas Little. Among Bunning's chief works may be mentioned Nunhead Cemetery, the Coal Exchange, Holloway Gaol, Billingsgate Market, and the Metropolitan Cattle Market at Copenhagen Fields near Pentonville. He died 'a victim to the bad organization of the city offices in the surveying and architectural department' at his residence, 6 Gloucester Terrace, Regent's Park, on 7 November 1863.[27] He was the city architect of London for some twenty years after he left the London Cemetery

The Egyptian Avenue in Highgate Cemetery
Nunhead Cemetery. Note the catacombs underneath

Company. His tomb, a simple slab on a podium, is on the circular road of the cemetry, and has a fine sense of dignity about it.

Highgate Cemetery has its fair share of London's illustrious dead, including George Eliot, Michael Faraday, and members of the Rossetti family. There was, however, probably nothing like the scene at Tom Sayers' funeral in 1865 anywhere. Sayers was a celebrated pugilist from the East End, whose untimely death was the occasion for an unofficial public holiday. Along the route of the procession, said a contemporary reporter, the publicans had lowered their window blinds and hung out craped flags. Photographic likenesses of the deceased were freely sold. At one public-house on the route might be seen seated at the open upper window a convivial party of ladies and gentlemen, the former with gin-and-water on their laps, cheerfully carolling Whitechapel ditties, while the latter joined in chorus, cracking walnuts at intervals. Presently there was a commotion amongst the mob, and a cry of '*it* comes' went up. 'It' was the black hearse. The chief mourner was a great brown dog! The bereaved animal occupied a mail-phaeton alone, and was attired in as deep mourning as the breadth of his collar, which was bound in black crape, would permit. A little way off was a ballad-singer chanting in praise of the deceased hero, and gathering halfpence from the throng. 'The ditty being set to a popular tune, many of the people about joined in chorus . . .' In they swarmed, the 'slow-eyed, great jawed multitude from the East, clattering over the gravel walks, trampling with their clinkered boots over delicate marble slabs, and playing leap-frog with every sepulchral monument of a convenient height that stood in their way'. The police were called to stop some deliberate vandalism by oafs seeking a good seat. Blasphemies were heard in profusion, and not even the pile of earth from the

[*98*]

grave was considered sacred, so it was commandeered as a ringside seat by several stalwarts.[28]

Julius Beer's Mausoleum, mentioned earlier, was designed by John Oldrid Scott and built of Portland stone from Messrs Giles's quarries. The crypt itself was entered

Julius Beer's mausoleum at Highgate, by John Oldrid Scott, 1877-8

from the lower catacombs. The sculpture was from the studio of Mr H. Hugh Armstead, ARA, and Mr Terry executed the marble sarcophagus. Farmer and Brindley were the carvers and modellers of the bronze door. The contractors were C. Millward and Co of Kentish Wharf, Thomas Leigh being clerk of works. The monument cost £5,000 (page 99).[19]

Highgate is also remembered for three exhumations. Elizabeth Siddall, wife of Dante Gabriel Rossetti, was disinterred one autumn night by the light of a great bonfire. Seven years before, Rossetti had placed the manuscript of his poems in the coffin with her. When the coffin was opened, the flames were reflected in the brilliance of Elizabeth's red-gold hair, which had grown in death and had covered her remains. The book was removed, and with it came several strands of hair. After the book had been disinfected and dried, it was returned to the author.

Karl Marx and his family, in the new part of the cemetery, were exhumed and re-interred in a spot beside the path. The grave is now covered by an enormous plinth and bust of singular ugliness.

The third exhumation was in 1907 when Mrs Druce claimed that T. C. Druce was really the Duke of Portland, and that T. C. Druce's coffin was empty. However, the coffin was indeed occupied, and the story died a natural death.[30]

Lloyd, writing in 1888, informs us that there were 25,000 graves in Highgate, each with four bodies per grave, totalling 100,000 bodies in all. Happily the soil is a stiff clay, he wrote, and no portion of the Fleet River or its effluents were used for domestic purposes, as it flows silently through the sewers. 'But the future of this cemetery is a matter of serious consideration for the neighbourhood, the earth becoming yearly more densely charged with the most poisonous

The strange, Italianate landscape of Highgate Cemetery

matter.'[31] Mr Lloyd thought that churchyards, though disgusting, were at least of limited size, but that the metropolitan cemeteries could be a great menace in the future. His fears have proved groundless, but there is a new threat to Highgate Cemetery, which has become remarkably overgrown. Indeed, nature has gone wild, and the 'Egyptian' catacombs are crumbling badly. The lush vegetation certainly adds atmosphere, and the 'pleasing melancholy' of it all is quite an experience, but many of the tombs have disappeared in the undergrowth. Is it too much to hope for that this astonishing Victorian necropolis, and others like it, may be saved from utter decay (page 97)? It would be a terrible mistake if the cemetery were to be demolished. However, some thinning of the vegetation, extensive weeding, and restoration of the crumbling plaster would help it enormously (page 96). This city of the dead is vulnerable, and we ought to think of preserving it almost intact as one of the most remarkable legacies of the Victorian age. Unfortunately the wider paths are now being partially filled in with common graves, and this contributes further to the over-

Plan of Nunhead Cemetery; showing the proposed sites of chapels, in accordance with the designs submitted by Thomas Little, architect. A note on the drawing says that the grounds were laid out by J. B. Bunning, and the chapels were erected by Thomas Little in 1844

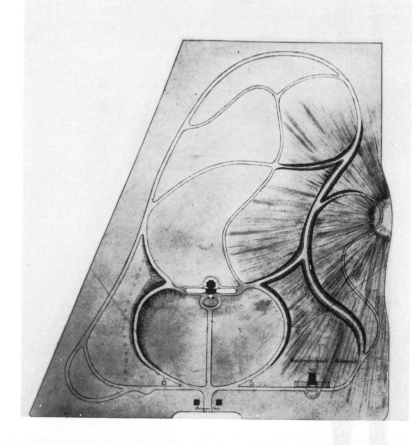

NUNHEAD . CEMETERY .

PLAN shewing the **PROPOSED SITES** of CHAPELS

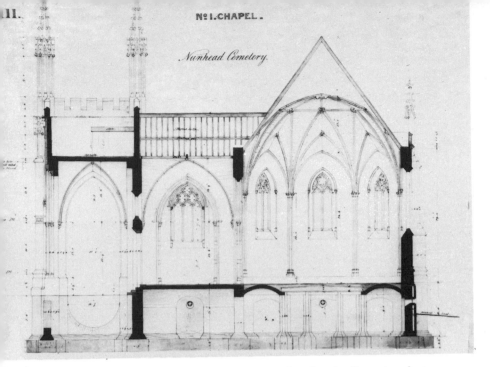

Sectional drawing of Thomas Little's designs for the Anglican chapel at Nunhead Cemetery. Note the catacombs underneath

crowded aspects and general chaos of this cemetery. Matters have become so serious that questions were asked in the House of Lords on 10 December 1970 by Lord Segal.[32]

Nunhead Cemetery

Geary's London Cemetery Company lost no time in setting out a second cemetery for the interment of the dead south of the river. This time, as at Highgate, a hill-top site was chosen—Nunhead near Peckham. The fifty acres of the Cemetery of All Saints were consecrated on 29 July 1840.[33] Today we can see how right Arnold Whittick was when he wrote that the 'cemeteries of London have contributed to the open spaces. Without them the urban sprawl might have become more unbroken. In the City, what valued spaces are the churchyards!' Mr Whittick added that cemeteries add

Thomas Little's drawings for Nunhead

dignity to our culture.[34] Nunhead forms a huge wedge of
open space, well planted with fine mature trees, in a particularly dismal part of London. Unfortunately many will regard
this cemetery as an eyesore, for at the time of writing it is
prone to savage attacks by vandals. The Dissenters' chapel
has been demolished, and the charming, light, and feathery
Anglican chapel is daily being reduced to a ruin. The catacombs have been broken into and coffins have been thrown
to the ground. Monuments have been smashed. Both gate

Little's Anglican chapel at Nunhead

lodges have been reduced to near dereliction. Similar damage is reported from Highgate (1971).

Nunhead was closed in 1969. In 1967 the London Cemetery Company was taken over by United Cemeteries Ltd. The registers for Nunhead and several items concerning Highgate were found abandoned in the cemetery. This astonishing callousness towards valuable historical records and the dereliction of the cemetery itself are only possible to understand when we remember that privately owned cemeteries are a residue of an extraordinary boom in early

Victorian times which came to a sudden end (see Chapter 6). What was not realised is that, since land is sold with rights in perpetuity, cemeteries must be a wasting asset. There can be no hope of profit, since local-authority cemeteries have the upper hand. The 500 acre cemetery at Brookwood is fairly profitable, but even there labour costs create difficulties in keeping it impeccable.

Nunhead Cemetery is of particular interest since it is Bunning's best-known layout. A competition was arranged for the design of the chapels, which seems to have been standard procedure, and this was won by Thomas Little in 1844. Born in February 1802, Little was a pupil of Robert Abraham. He designed St Mark's, Regent's Park, in 1848; All Saints, St John's Wood, in 1850; St Saviour's, Paddington, in 1856. The Nunhead works were carried out under Little's supervision, and are in chaste Gothic. The complete drawings survive in the Drawings Collection of the Royal Institute of British Architects (pages 102-5). Little died at 36 Northumberland Street, Marylebone Road, on 20 December 1859.[35] Pevsner, in *London*, volume 2 of *The Buildings of England* series, incorrectly attributes the chapels and entrance with lodges to Bunning.

Abney Park Cemetery

Abney Park Cemetery has already been mentioned in connection with J. C. Loudon, who admired the planting. The cemetery at Stoke Newington was opened by the Lord Mayor on 20 May 1840 and comprised some thirty-five acres. The Abney Park Cemetery Company had its offices at the cemetery in rather unusual Egyptian lodges with striking entrance gates. Apart from these magnificent gates, there is an oddly mean-looking chapel in cardboard Gothic (page 107), and a rather fine statue of Isaac Watts, who stayed at the house which formerly occupied the site (page 108).

The 'oddly mean-looking chapel in cardboard Gothic' at Abney Park Cemetery, by William Hosking

The architect for Abney Park was Professor William Hosking, born in Buckfastleigh on 26 November 1800. He went to Australia in his early years and was apprenticed there. He returned in 1819, and in 1820 was articled to Mr Jenkins of London. In 1834 he became engineer to the Birmingham, Bristol, and Thames Junction Railway, designing the portion near All Souls Cemetery, Kensal Green. He became professor at King's College, London, and laid out Abney Park in 1839-43. He died on 2 August 1861 at

The monument to Isaac Watts at Abney Park Cemetery. It is by Baily

23 Woburn Square.[36] The sculptor for Dr Watts's monument was Mr Baily, who, according to *The Builder*, was commissioned to carry out the work.[37]

There are few monuments apart from that to Dr Watts of any interest in Abney Park, and much reuse of land appears to be taking place at the time of writing. However, the excellent planting is now a delight, and a lesson to us how well the nineteenth century understood the juxtaposition of trees and monuments. Abney Park is also threatened with change (1971).

Tower Hamlets Cemetery

Tower Hamlets Cemetery, off the Mile End Road, was established at the same time as Abney Park Cemetery by the City of London and Tower Hamlets Cemetery Company. The area was originally some thirty acres. It was consecrated in 1841. The last burial was in 1966, and it was acquired by the Greater London Council in that year. The cemetery was hit by bombs during the war, and it is difficult to visualise what the chapels and catacombs were like. The grounds are astonishing, however, for here again nature has gone wild, and forests of tombstones from the mid-nineteenth century vie with forests of trees, only to lose the battle. The density of burial must be very high indeed, and the place has a curious air of Cockney togetherness even in death. Tower Hamlets Cemetery seems to have become overgrown soon after its establishment, for Mrs Basil Holmes reported in 1896 that it was 'utterly neglected'.

The City of London and Tower Hamlets Cemetery Company appears to have been in trouble financially too. A General Bill from Templer, Shearman & Slater, solicitors, of 23 Great Tower Street caused the directors great concern as it was almost for one thousand pounds, but the firm's total bill for all the legal work leading up to the completion of the cemetery was for over three thousand pounds. The architect to the company is referred to in the Bills as 'Mr. Brandon', of the firm of Wyatt and Brandon. The drainage schemes for the new land acquired in the 1850s were by Henry George Haywood, engineer.[38]

Now that several of these private-enterprise cemeteries are in a state of decay, nature is reported to be winning. Foxes have been seen in both Highgate and Nunhead, and wild life of all sorts is being studied by naturalists. It has even been suggested that vampires inhabit the catacombs, and several people have reported seeing ghosts.[39] Rumour had it that the Russians were going to buy Highgate, but this has been discounted.

The General Cemetery Company still operates Kensal Green, and a large crematorium has added to business. The catacombs by the Harrow Road and the Dissenters' chapel are in poor state of repair, and much of the ground is overgrown. Yet neither the catacombs nor the Dissenters' chapel is used, so the company no doubt has a duty to the shareholders not to use money repairing the property. The United Cemeteries Ltd at the time of writing own Nunhead and Highgate,[40] and the Ministry of Public Building and Works owns Brompton. Norwood has been taken over by Lambeth Borough Council.

The private-enterprise cemeteries formed in the 1830s and 1840s were the first phase in the development of the London cemeteries, and are characterised by a mixture of grandeur and romanticism in their treatment. Their celebrity was short-lived, for more agitation together with financial difficulties contributed to their decline. It is to this new phase that we now turn.

The first private enterprise cemetery to be taken over by the Government

Too late the wished-for boon has come,
Too late wiped out the stain,—
No Schedule shall restore to health,
No Act give life again
To the thousands whom, in bygone years,
Our City Graves have slain!

'City Graves'. An anonymous poem from
Household Words, 14 December 1850

THE WEST OF LONDON & Westminster Cemetery Company can be credited with the building of the most formal of all the great London cemeteries. Although not consecrated until 15 June 1840, it has a long history of great interest to this study. Situated at Brompton, it is frequently referred to as the Brompton Cemetery.

The company was first advertised in 1836, but up to 1837, when the Bill of Incorporation was introduced to the House of Commons, few subscriptions had been received. There was opposition in the Lords based upon the experiences of clergy working the General Cemetery Company's Cemetery at Kensal Green, for they wished to protect themselves against the loss of burial fees. After Kensal Green the next application to Parliament was from the South Metropolitan Cemetery Company, and by that bill a fee of one guinea was imposed on all interments. The West of London & Westminster Cemetery Company's Bill of Incorporation reduced the fee to ten shillings.

On 5 July 1837 agreement was reached to purchase about forty acres from Lord Kensington. The Act obtained the Royal Assent on 15 July 1837,[1] but certain family difficulties delayed completion.

Stephen Geary, whose address is given as 10 Hamilton Place, was appointed architect to the West of London and Westminster Cemetery Company on 20 July 1837.[2] His duties were to be the carrying out of all works ordered by the board, his remuneration being $2\frac{1}{2}$ per cent on work completed. The capital of the company was increased to £100,000, and by early 1838 negotiations were under way with Lord Kensington and with the Equitable Gas Company for the purchase of land. It was decided to offer premiums by advertisement for the best designs for the walls, chapels, catacombs, and buildings of the Cemetery, a hundred guineas for the best design, fifty guineas for the second, and twenty-

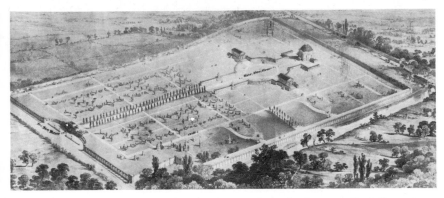

Baud's design for Brompton Cemetery. Note the Roman Catholic and Nonconformist chapels facing each other across the Great Circle. The Old Brompton Road entrance is on the left, in the arcaded wall. In the foreground is the long line of catacombs

five guineas for the third. Geary himself was eligible to enter the competition. On 3 July a Committee was to frame the competition advertisement, it having been reported that 'Advertising for Plans was not contrary to Etiquette'.[3] By 31 July tenders had been received for the wall round the cemetery, three of which were submitted to the architect for valuation. On 7 August it was resolved to accept the tender of Messrs Robert and George Webb.

At a meeting held on 5 December 1837 it was decided to appoint Mr Ramsay landscape gardener. Ramsay must have worked closely with Geary, for he landscaped Highgate as well. G. F. Carden approached the board on 2 November with offers of advice and experience of cemeteries, but he declined a directorship. The board wrote to Carden thanking him, but regretted that they were unable to entertain his suggestions.

On 7 September 1838 the board was to constitute a 'Committee of Taste to sit . . . for the examination of the Designs', for on 5 September the plans had been opened

[*113*]

and examined.[4] On 20 September it was reported that the Committee of Taste had awarded the first premium to 'Windsor', and five days later the board made the awards subject to confirmation 'after consultation with Practical Men'. Mr Shaw was requested to advise the board in this matter.

The awards were confirmed on 2 October. First premium was awarded to Mr Benjamin Baud; second premium to Messrs H. E. Kendall (already mentioned with regard to Kensal Green) and Thomas Allom (who designed a mausoleum in Norwood); and third premium to Mr Frederick Sang.

It was decided on 7 January 1839 that the directors would submit to a General Meeting on 10 January a resolution calling for the cancellation of Geary's appointment as architect unless they received an intimation of his resignation. So far Geary had received £221 8s 6d for his services. Geary tendered his resignation, and it was accepted, for at this time he was probably very much involved with the London Cemetery Company, and now that Baud had won the competition it was clear his position would be untenable.

However, there may have been other difficulties, for it was clear that there was trouble over the monies paid to Geary, the argument being that architects were paid by percentage of work done. Geary then asked for compensation as the 'projector' of the cemetery, and the company wrote to him hoping that he would see the propriety of not pursuing the matter. It was suggested that Geary had erred in his calculations of the size of the cemetery, the actual area being smaller than that estimated. Geary's solicitors then wrote to the company asking for £498 4s, but the board denied any liability. The board decided to offer Geary £100 'without prejudice', which he rejected, then bringing an action against the company for £449. The board paid £90 16s 6d to the court. On 9 December 1840 the solicitor explained the causes which had led to the postponement of the trial of Geary's action, the 'cause having been struck out of the Paper'. On 1 December 1841 it was reported that £162 had been paid over Geary's action.

On 19 February 1839 it was resolved to accept the 'General Designs of Mr. Baud in its main elements and order of Architecture adopted for the buildings of the Company subject to any modifications in detail or extent that may seem expedient'.[5] Benjamin J. Baud, architect, a pupil of Francis Goodwin, who had designed a cemetery to be sited on Primrose Hill, was assistant to Sir Jeffry Wyatville when he took an active part in the alterations and improvements at Windsor Castle. He entered the RA Schools in 1829, and exhibited RA 1826-51. He published a work in 1842, with Michael Gandy, called *Architectural Illustrations of Windsor Castle*, with historical accounts by John Britton, and his pseudonym in the competition for Brompton Cemetery reflects his connection with Wyatville and the alterations. He spent many of his last years 'painting in oils or preparing drawings'. 'The promises of his early years were scarcely fulfilled.'[6] He died at Richmond, aged 69, on 17 April 1875.

The Builder obituary suggests a rather lonely, forgotten man. It is worth examining the situation to see just what did happen. The story is a tragic one, for it is that of a young man producing a design of genius and then falling foul of the board for financial reasons. Brompton Cemetery, in fact, practically ended Baud's promising career.

In February 1839 the secretary wrote to Sir Jeffry Wyatville to 'inquire as to the competency of Mr. Baud to carry out works shown as his design'. Baud was then appointed the architect to carry out the building, subject to an agreement to be made with him as to the terms upon which he would supervise the works. His remuneration was to be 5 per cent of outlay excluding the cost of the wall. A plan of the ground ordered by the Act was to be made by Baud free of cost. Baud waived his claim to the premium, and on 20 February he was ordered to prepare estimates and drawings of his design, the cost not to exceed £30,000.

By April Baud was making specifications for the lodge, and advertisements were placed for tenders for bricklayers', masons' and smiths' work for the north and the east boundary walls. On 30 April the board accepted Mr John Faulkner's tender for the boundary walls. On 6 August it was ordered that Baud should place at the disposal of the clerk of works not more than six men for preliminary work. The tenders for the lodge were advertised, and on 20 August the tender for the masonry, brickwork, and artificers' work for the north wall and lodge was given to Messrs Nowell, and it was resolved that these contractors should begin work at once, the stone to be Aisleby. At the same time changes were ordered for the design of the catacombs, 3in York-stone covers being substituted for brick arches.[7]

The company advertised for a landscape gardener, and on 15 October 'Mr. Finamore', 'late gardener to Lord Ravensworth and Normanby', was appointed to the company at a salary of £2 per week. 'Finamore' (actually Isaac Finnemore) worked closely with Baud in carrying out the planting, and the result is a landscape of restraint with pleasant shaded walks, especially on the east and south. In December 1839 it was minuted that none other than J. C. Loudon had offered his advice on the planting, at a fee, of course, and it was agreed to pay him ten guineas for his professional opinions, the company clearly being anxious to get the best possible team together for the planting. It seems that while Loudon gave advice and Finnemore was employed by the company, Ramsay supplied plants and materials, for he is recorded as still carrying out works for the company long after Finnemore's appointment. Ramsay had a nurseryman's business

[*116*]

in Brompton, and it seems that he was not strictly speaking an employee of the company.

On 1 October 1839 it was 'resolved that the Planting and laying out of the Grounds of the Cemetery be performed by a hired Gardener, made under the immediate superintendance of the Architect, and not by the employment of a Landscape Gardener'. Finnemore resigned his position on 29 July 1840, probably because he was being paid with shares.

Early in 1840 a special meeting was announced to consider the architect's report with reference to his recommendation that a decision be made on the erection of the chapels. The architect prepared plans and estimates for a temporary chapel. In February Baud was asked to convert the lodge into a temporary chapel, and money problems were reported, it being resolved to raise £30,000 by borrowing.

On 15 March Baud was ordered to prepare a specification for the chapel as originally designed, but without catacombs underneath. Baud did this, and his drawing shows 'Buildings without the Catacombs the brick piers being carried down to enable the Company to build Graves, Vaults or Catacombs hereafter'. Baud's designs for the centre gate of the lodge were approved, and it was decided to construct the roof of the chapel of cast iron and to cover it with lead. The chapel was to be built of Bath stone. On 29 April Baud submitted drawings and estimates of the carcass of the chapel, the tenders to be delivered by 20 May. Messrs Nowell got the job. At the same time Mr Gutch, surveyor of Paddington, reported that deeper drains were required. A clerk and sexton, and a chaplain were also appointed in May. The minutes say the consecration was fixed for Friday 12 June at 3 o'clock, but *The Times* reports the consecration as having taken place on 15 June.

On 8 July Baud was ordered to prepare a drawing of a small monument to be erected over the grave of Mrs C.

Bell Tower above the catacombs, Brompton Cemetery

Boyle Shaw and he produced two designs on 10 July. Mrs Shaw's body was the first to be interred, and the gravestone is a flat slab from which all lettering has long since vanished. The architect was required to suggest in what way he would recommend the board to 'expend £13,000 towards the completion of his design'. Originally the motion said that he should revise his estimates so that a final sum would not be in excess of £25,000. The architect prepared estimates and working drawings for more economical versions of the Great Circle and Bell Towers.

At the Annual General Meeting of 8 February 1841 it was stated that the boundary walls, lodge and entrance, and catacombs attached to the west wall were all finished before June 1840, when consecration took place. Since that time, a public vault had been completed as well as the external work of the principal chapel, and considerable progress was being made with the other buildings which formed the 'prominent features in the Architect's design'.[8] However, the original capital had been wholly insufficient to meet the expenditure required for completing the cemetery buildings. It was decided to raise money by issuing 1,000 new shares, and to abandon the idea of borrowing the money. On 17 February Messrs Nowell's tender of £2,193 for finishing the interior of the chapel was accepted, and in the following month it was decided that it would be desirable to complete the Great Circle, the shelters of the two chapels, the junction with the bell towers and some of the arcades, but without any more catacombs.[9]

A Special General Meeting was held on 17 May, when the financial problems of the company were discussed. The disorderly appearance caused by the fact that building was being carried out in bits and pieces was discouraging the public from making use of the cemetery. Baud produced a plan showing how the basic features of the design could be retained and part of the original design completed within the monies available. In June he reported that Messrs Nowell had completed two quarters of the Great Circle and bell towers 'agreeable with his drawings, etc'. On 21 July it was ordered that Messrs Drewer be instructed to supply two pairs of iron doors for the entrances to the catacombs in the Great Circle.[10] These were duly made and are splendid specimens decorated with the suitable symbols of inverted torches, serpents, and hourglasses.

At the Annual General Meeting in February 1842 the directors were considering adapting the cemetery chapel for public worship, but this was abandoned. There was a general opinion that the terms demanded by the Sewer Authorities should not have been required of the company. It was reported that patronage 'hitherto bestowed by the public' was limited 'owing to the want of the quiet and repose which are, in every mind, associated with a Cemetery'.

One year later, a serious financial situation was revealed. Already, the directors were giving much attention to make arrangements to reduce expenditure on the maintenance of the cemetery. By 1 March it was clear that there was trouble between the company and its architect in connection with the report of a Mr Wiskin who was called in as arbitrator. Clearly Baud was not being paid and was in fact owed £1,436 4s. In 1842 the directors had reduced salaries and wages, and there was obviously no money available, the landscaper and others being 'paid' in shares.

In the minutes for 25 February 1844 there is evidence that Baud was no longer acting as architect, for we learn that a drawing made by Mr Winterbottom of Waltham Green, surveyor, of a proposed new entrance to the cemetery had been submitted to the company. On 13 March 1844 it was resolved to 'remove Mr. Baud from the office of Architect'. A letter was sent on behalf of Baud from E. Naylor, noting that the company had employed Messrs Winterbottom and Sands to make drawings for a lodge and for the removal of gates. The letter asked why Baud had not been applied to first. Baud wrote that he had already furnished the directors with two designs and estimates for a lodge at the Fulham end of the cemetery. On 3 April a letter from Naylor on behalf of Baud was sent, which stated that Baud had asked

The Anglican chapel at Brompton

the directors if they were satisfied with him, to which he received unanimous approval. The letter asked for a Special Meeting, to investigate any charges.

In 1843 there were serious defects noted in the roof of the West Catacombs, but this was due to the work not being carried out in conformity with the architect's specification. Nowell's were asked for an explanation, to which they replied that the company's architect had passed the work. An action against Nowell's was brought, and the company was awarded £300 damages. Baud was nevertheless removed from office, and he brought an action in April 1844 for £4,000 which came to trial on 23 June 1846, according to

[*121*]

the minutes of the company, now in the Public Record Office. *The Times* reported that on 12 February 1846 at the Court of the Exchequer, in the case of *Band* [sic] v *The West London Cemetery Company*, so few of the jurymen turned up that the Lord Chief Baron, Sir F. J. Porlock, of Serjeants' Inn, directed that all absentees should be fined. On 20 May 1846 Baud offered to refer his claim to arbitration, but since the company had offered just that the previous November and Baud had refused, it now turned down Baud's request.

The trial on 23 June, before the Lord Chief Baron of the Court of Exchequer, was a disaster for Baud. His Lordship 'pronounced in favor [*sic*] of the validity of the agreement entered into between Mr. Baud and the Coy. as to the terms on which he was to serve the Coy. and expressed his opinion that according to the terms of such agreement Mr. Baud is not entitled to charge the Coy. for plans and drawings furnished by him for buildings which have not yet been carried out'.

'At this state of the proceedings', state the minutes for 1 July 1846, p 465, the advisability of an offer on the part of the defendants to withdraw a 'Juror on each party paying the costs incurred on either side was suggested to the Solicitor by the Company's leading counsel, that himself and the Chairman having concurred in the adoption of such a course, the offer was accordingly made to which the Plaintiff consented on condition that the same should be without prejudice to any claim which he might think proper to pursue against the Coy. in the event of any of the, at present, unused plans and drawings furnished by him being adopted in further carrying out the Buildings at any future period'.

From the minutes of 11 November[11] we learn that it was resolved that a draft be drawn in favour of Messrs Macdougall & Upton for £200 on account for the 'Coy's costs in Mr. Baud's action', and that they be requested to pay the balance of the charges of the professional witnesses. This balance was £134 2s. A perfunctory note in the minutes for 3 February 1847 refers to 'expenses' of the action by B. Baud. At the Annual General Meeting a few days later (p 476) it was stated that 'the Coys. expenses were heavy', in Baud's action. The parallel between Geary's action and Baud's is obvious.

Baud seems to have specialised in the production of paintings and drawings after 1846, and there is a reference in *The Builder* to his work for private clients in the domestic architecture field. He appears to have designed several villas in and around London and to have carried out alteration and improvement work for wealthy clients. An increased interest in painting, probably encouraged by the unfortunate experiences over Brompton Cemetery, where he was unable to complete his grand, formal scheme besides having difficulty in getting paid for his work, consoled him in his last years. Partially paralysed from a stroke sustained in the 1870s, he died in 1875 and received only the shortest of obituaries.

After 1846 the company continued in the doldrums. Dividends were small, and debts were large. Attempts were constantly being made to economise, and as a result the maintenance of the grounds and fabric was poor. The catacombs had filled up early, but by 1850 it was clear that Baud's formal conception would have to be sacrificed to a dense use of the ground for burial.

Further problems arose, for at the Annual General Meeting of 20 January 1851 the directors were anxiously watching the changes arising from the passing of the Metropolitan Interments Act. The experiment of establishing commercial cemeteries was not widely followed after 1850. Up to then the idea was favourably viewed, and in 1847 a Cemetery Clauses Act was passed, the purpose of which was to supply general rules applicable to all public companies which might establish cemeteries in the future.[12] Shortly afterwards, owing to agitation which will be described later, there was a change of outlook. A Parliamentary Report said that interment of the dead was a most unfit subject for commercial speculation, and in 1850 an Act of Parliament[13] constituted a Metropolitan Burial District and granted the General Board of Health power to provide burial grounds and to purchase the commercial cemeteries which had already been established. In fact, only one, Brompton, was acquired, and the Act was repealed in 1852, when the Vestries were empowered to establish Burial Boards.[14]

It was apparent that the Metropolitan Interments Act could hit the private companies hard, and the directors of the West of London & Westminster Cemetery Company prayed in a petition that the Bill should be referred to a Select Committee. It was, however, impossible for the company to petition against the principle of the Bill, namely the counteraction of the evils arising from intramural interments, though the relevant clauses gave inadequate compensation to individuals who had sunk their capital in undertakings which the Bill proposed to outlaw. The Bill was passed in spite of opposition, and received the Royal Assent on 5 August 1850.

In September the directors received a letter from the General Board of Health to say that a valuation was to be made in contemplation of a possible purchase. In March 1851, in a letter from Chadwick, it was stated that the Board of Health had a valuation, and it was suggested that the company also should prepare a valuation. On 19 March the company's secretary laid before the board an account of the total expenditure on capital, which came to £147,685 7s 2d. Included in this account is the sum of £3,203 7s for 'architects and surveyors', and £4,185 1s for 'salaries of officers'.

The main entrance to Brompton Cemetery

It seems, therefore, that Baud got some, if not all, of his money. The board of directors said they would not be satisfied with a sum less than that actually expended. There appear to have been squabbles over the amount of money to be agreed in a financial settlement, and on 23 April 1851 a letter was dispatched from the Board of Health stating that it was intended to summon a jury to settle and assess the sum to be paid for the cemetery. The board were offering £43,836. A Special General Meeting of the company rejected this on 28 April, and it was resolved to ask £166,762 12s 8d from the board. By 23 July the dispute was submitted to arbitration, and on 30 October Barnes Peacock, Esq, the umpire, awarded a sum of £74,921 14s, although 'circumstances have taken place that create some expectation that other schemes are now under the consideration of persons in authority for the completion of which it will not be necessary to purchase the Cemeteries and that they are inclined to propose that each party forego the award'.

At the Special General Meeting of 27 December 1851 a letter from the Board of Health was read in which they proposed that the award be abandoned, the board to pay the legal costs, but on 26 January a motion was passed by the company's Special General Meeting that the directors should enforce the award. On 28 January 1852 the directors called upon the Board of Health to fulfil the terms of the contract, there being clauses in the new Act which safeguarded the company's legal right to have their purchase completed. On 1 September the solicitor reported that the purchase of the company's property was imminent, and on 27 October the purchase money was placed at the disposal of the Chief Commissioner of HM Works & Public Buildings. On 5 November it was resolved to pay each shareholder ten guineas forthwith, and on 24 August 1853 a second instalment of 16s per share was paid out of the purchase money. The balance left was divided among the shareholders, at 3s 5d per share. 20 December 1854 saw the final meeting of the Company. Brompton Cemetery is now administered by the Ministry of Public Building and Works as successors to the Victorian body.

The cemetery is laid out on a strong axis from the Old Brompton Road to the Fulham Road. The purchase of land on the Fulham Road was never completed, and so the main entrance was the triumphal arch on the Old Brompton Road. A high brick wall surrounds the cemetery, and it is arcaded on the Old Brompton Road frontage. A main avenue leads from the gates to the huge octagonal chapel, the dome of which dominates the vista. The long arms of the catacombs, one of which has a bell tower (page 118), reach out in an embrace round the Great Circle, and a long range of catacombs lies against the western wall of the cemetery.

The main entrance is a triumphal gateway incorporating

The monument to Coombes at Brompton

the lodges which recalls Kensal Green (page 125). The axis
which is straddled by this gateway runs through the Anglican
chapel. The conception is magnificent, and it is tragic the
design was never completed, for originally there were to
have been three chapels: the Anglican one being the domed
octagonal structure which exists and dominates (page 121);
and two other chapels opposite each other, on either side of
the Great Circle, for Roman Catholics and Dissenters. The

bird's-eye view of Baud's design shows the grandeur of the scheme in its entirety, before the Great Circle became cluttered up with densely packed tombs, many of which are poor in terms of design (page 113).

However, the cemetery possesses some early tombs to the south of the chapel which are classically simple, while several rather grand mausolea and one curious tomb of copper, bronze, and stone catch the eye (page 121). There are few examples in Brompton as fine as those in either Norwood or Kensal Green, however, and generally the tombs are disappointing. *The Builder* castigated the monument of Coombes,[15] the champion sculler, depicting an upturned skiff (page 127), and described it as 'bad and vulgar, so ugly as a whole, so execrable in the details'. Jackson, the pugilist, had an altar-tomb with athlete-figures, modelled by Baily, who also executed Isaac Watts's statue

Brompton Cemetery, from an indigo-wash drawing by William Cowen. Stamford Bridge is on the right

in Abney Park.[16] *The Builder* did, however, illustrate some tombs of which it approved, including one by Ashpitel on 5 January 1867. The formality of the layout and the shady walks by family vaults built by the eastern wall of the cemetery provide moments of great aesthetic pleasure.

Shortly after the cemetery had been completed, William Cowen made an indigo wash of the prospect from the canal. This shows the very rural setting in which the cemetery was conceived, and it appears almost like a walled city in the midst of the country, the great dome of the Anglican chapel and the two bell towers rising up above the long rows of colonnaded catacombs (page 128). The canal is now occupied by the District Line railway.

6 The campaign against intramural interment

Hark! cracks the mattock on a coffin lid,
And earth gives up her injured dead, unbid.

The Cemetery, *1848*

Agitation and Controversy

The several cemeteries in the suburbs were the property of Joint Stock Companies, apart from Brompton Cemetery, which had been acquired by the Board of Health in 1852. From the costliness of interment in them, they only went a small way towards abating the problems of intramural burial. As the cities grew and the cemeteries, which only a few years earlier had been in the country, became surrounded by houses, the extent of the problem was realised. In particular, the difficulties of disposing of the dead from the poorer classes had not been solved, and individuals still made money by operating burial places.

G. F. Carden's agitation in the *Penny Magazine* had largely helped to create the climate of opinion in which Kensal Green was established. However, between 1835 and 1855 attention was drawn in the press and in parliamentary committees to the continuing horrific state of the churchyards, and this chapter will discuss this second wave of agitation which was to end intramural interment and involve public authorities in the formation of cemeteries.

On 8 March 1842 a committee of the House of Commons was appointed which uncovered a state of things in London truly described as 'sickening'. In that year there were 218 acres of intramural burial grounds in London. It was computed that 44,355 bodies were buried in them per annum.[1] Interest in the problem at official level had been stimulated by the journalism of George Frederick Carden, but it was George Alfred Walker's *Gatherings from Grave-Yards* of 1839 which revealed the situation in all its detail to an astounded nation. *Gatherings from Grave-Yards, particularly those of London; with a concise History of the Modes of Interment among different Nations, from the earliest Periods; and a Detail of dangerous and fatal Results produced by the unwise and revolting Custom of inhuming the Dead in the midst of the Living* was reviewed by the *Gardener's Magazine* 'conducted' by J. C. Loudon in vol 16 of 1840. 'As gardeners are frequently called on to lend their assistance in laying out cemeteries, they also ought to peruse it', wrote Loudon.

The Builder[2] denounced churchyards in favour of cemeteries, quoting Père-la-Chaise and other Parisian examples. Mr Mackinnon gave notice that on 18th inst he would call the attention of the House to the necessity of improving the health of towns by preventing burial of the dead within their precincts.[3] In the same volume, on p 92, a letter from the celebrated C. A. Walker referred to a previous report[4] in which he described Spa Fields Burial Ground and the practice of burning coffins and human remains there, and the 'tremendous stench' that came from such burning. A week later the manager of Spa Fields wrote to say proceedings would be taken against C. A. Walker,[5] but, undeterred, the gallant surgeon, in a letter dated 19 February 1845, went on to elaborate his denunciations of burial in towns on grounds of health and decency, and to ask pertinent questions about open graves, length of decay, depth of burial, and other matters.[6] A report was published stating that an intolerable stench from Spa Fields caused complaints to be made to the magistrates. Sparks and smoke were noted coming from the bone house, and human flesh had been seen to be carried to the furnace. There had been two deaths from 'putrid fever'.[7] *Household Words* published a long poem called 'City Graves' on 14 December 1850 which contained a verse which summed up the state of the churchyards:

> I saw from out the earth peep forth
> The white and glistening bones,
> With jagged ends of coffin planks,
> That e'en the worm disowns;
> And once a smooth round skull rolled on,
> Like a football, on the stones.

[*132*]

Sir James Graham spoke in the House of Commons of the growing feeling of public opinion against the practices being employed to make room in the churchyards. *The Builder* praised G. A. Walker for his efforts, and spoke of 'Mr Mackinnon's long expected motion for preventing interment in large towns'.[8] The House of Commons came to the conclusion that the practice of interment in large cities was 'injurious to health'.[9] There was a letter in *The Builder* on the state of the graveyards of Southwark,[10] and a spate of correspondence followed all through 1845. Public opinion was swinging well behind the reformers, however, and when the Enon Chapel affair was reported, a scandal ensued, despite the assertion that the Bishop of London enjoyed excellent health because he lived in Bishopsgate Churchyard.

Spa Fields had no space left, but you could 'always get a grave there'.[11] Knight said that the 'age of miracles seems to have revived with regard to many of the burial grounds'.[12] 'But all the marvels of the churchyard must give place to those performed in connection with Enon Chapel.' This building, situated in Clement's Lane, in the Strand, was built by the minister himself (a Dissenter) as a speculation. The upper part, opened for public worship in 1823, was separated from the lower only by a boarded floor; and in this space (about 60ft by 29ft, and 6ft deep) 12,000 bodies were estimated to have been interred.[13] Quicklime was used to hasten the destruction of the flesh, and the coffins were removed by the chapel staff and burnt. In fact, in many of the choked burial grounds it was common practice to burn coffins and to destroy bodies with lime, such was the overcrowding.[14] Fox, custodian of the graveyard of St Anne's, Soho, made a substantial profit out of stripping lead, handles, nails, and screws from coffins. The smells were atrocious, by all accounts, and gravediggers were 'drunkards by force'.[15]

Mr Mackinnon ordered a prosecution to be commenced

[*133*]

over Spa Fields, and inquiries were made concerning Enon Chapel. He praised Chadwick's report but believed that the adoption of the measures recommended by Chadwick, including the abolition of all private interments and the undertaking of all burials by the government, would be repudiated by the country. Contrary to popular belief, he denied that the Church was opposed to reform.[16] Mr Bernal recommended Sir James Graham to close the cemeteries of the parishes of St Clement and St Anne. Dr Bowring said other countries had adopted cemeteries outside the towns and that the clergy were opposed to similar moves in Britain because of loss of fees, therefore he proposed compensation as a means of getting over this difficulty. Lord Mahon said that no question was more essential to the health of large towns than that which Mr Mackinnon had laid before the House. 'Better ventilation and draining of large towns were but trifles in comparison with the reforms suggested by Mr Mackinnon.'[17] The Earl of Lincoln urged caution.

The counsel for the Crown frustrated the action over Spa Fields, and *The Builder* sympathised with Mr G. A. Walker, whose evidence was criticised most severely.[18] A few days later Mr Atkinson, a surgeon, of Westminster, wrote to *The Lancet* about the mephitic state of St Margaret's churchyard and about the illnesses, fainting, and nausea experienced by many who breathed the gases.[19] On 27 October 1845 'Z' wrote that the interests of the clergy were intent on keeping the *status quo*, and he contrasted the city churchyards with Brompton, Kensal Green, and Norwood Cemeteries.[20]

In *The Builder* for 1846, we read that Mr J. R. Hamilton was the successful candidate in the Birmingham Cemetery competition. Other cemeteries already established were mentioned, including the Glasgow Necropolis, Dublin, Cork, Norwood, Abney Park, Kensal Green, Liverpool, Bath, Bristol, Cambridge, Gravesend, Kidderminster, Leeds,

Manchester, and Newcastle.[21] On the next page it was announced that Mr J. (*sic*, presumably G.) A. Walker would deliver the first of a series of lectures on the conditions of graveyards in London, their injurious consequences to public health and public morality, at the London Mechanics Institution, Chancery Lane. This lecture was widely praised later.[22]

J. D. Parry, writing in June 1846, mentioned the well-kept grounds of St Andrew, Holborn (Gray's Inn Road); St Pancras; St Giles-in-the-Fields (adjoining St Pancras); St Martin-in-the-Fields (Camden Town); St James, Piccadilly (Hampstead Road); and St Marylebone (St John's Wood),[23] and contrasted them with Spa Fields and other places.

The Builder considered Mr Mackinnon much too yielding when he permitted his Public Cemeteries Bill to be withdrawn on the understanding that its principles would be adopted by the government in the next session.[24] Controversy raged through 1847. *The Builder* said that the government would prohibit the use of overcrowded burial grounds.[25] G. A. Walker was again active, and J. D. Parry published *Urban Burial* about the state of the London graveyards. Sir W. Somerville and Sir George Grey brought in the Cemeteries Clauses Bill to stop burial under any cemetery chapel or within a certain distance of the outer wall of such a chapel, and to prevent bodies being buried in any grave not being a catacomb or vault at less than 30in from the surface to the upper side of the coffin. The Bill also provided for density of burial to be controlled as well as introducing penalties for defacing monuments.

On 27 August 1847 a meeting was held in the theatre of the Scientific Institution, Leicester Square, with Mr W. A. Mackinnon in the chair. All the details of the state of the graveyards of London were gone into again, and Mr G. A. Walker was once more praised for his efforts.[26] There was

[*135*]

also a meeting at the Crown and Anchor Tavern in the Strand to petition parliament to abolish burial in towns, Mr B. B. Cabbell, MP, presiding. The sagas of Enon and Elim chapels were again told. The result was that the Burial Authority for the Metropolis was constituted, empowered to close intramural churchyards; to lay out new cemeteries to the suburbs; and to take over others where necessary,[27] some eight years after the publication of *Gatherings*, and five years after the appointment of the Select Committee 'to inquire into Intra-Mural Sepulture and the Effect of Interment of Bodies on the Health of Towns'.

There were publications produced in plenty for and against the proposed legislation. One of the most curious of these was *The Cemetery. A brief appeal to the feelings of Society on Behalf of Extra Mural Burial.*[28] A quotation of some of the choicest passages will serve to illustrate the point. The work begins:

Hark! cracks the mattock on a coffin lid,
And earth gives up her injured dead, unbid.
Wrought loose as mole-hill 'neath th'oft ent'ring tools,
Each opening grave, a banquet meet for Ghoules,
Bids yawn in livid heaps the quarried flesh;
The plague-swoln charnel spreads its taint afresh.

The poet warms to his subject, and indignation waxes:

In foul accumulation, tier on tier,
Each due instalment of the pauper bier,
Crushed in dense-pack'd corruption there they dwell,
'Mongst earthy rags of shroud, and splinter'd shell.
A quagmire of old bones, where darkly bred,
The slimy life is busy with the dead.
Reeks from that bloated earth miasma's breath,
The full-fed taint of undigested death,
Thence, like the fumes from sleeping glutton's throat,
The noisome vapours of her surfeit float.

[*136*]

He contrasts such horrors with his demand that we:

> Turn hence, where death no persecution knows,
> Where dissolution's aspect is repose.
> Where sleep the rustic congregation, laid
> Around the holy walls where late they pray'd,

in order to imagine the country churchyard. But where there are large populations in cities, the picture could be a different one:

> But here her weeds let pensive nature wear,
> In sable cypress wrap the white tomb's glare;
> Bid ivied sorrows weep from ev'ry wall,
> And sunbeams melt to twilight as they fall.
> Let on grey stones the wild Virginian vine,
> Like graces bright'ning on a death-bed shine;
> Hue by hue rip'ning, loveliest at the last,
> A wreath of glory over ruin cast.
> Let plumy pine with cedar blend, and yew,
> To tuft the walk, and fringe the avenue:
> But oh! let love be first, and second art,
> Let Cemeteries win the people's heart;
> Though lowly lay secure the weary head,
> And in the tomb domesticate the dead.

Yet there had been tremendous opposition to the setting up of the Select Committee. A vicious attack was made by the Committee for opposing the Bill for the 'Improvement of Health in Towns' in a pamphlet entitled *Health of Towns. An examination of the Report and Evidence of the Select Committee; of Mr. MacKinnon's* [sic] *Bill and of the Acts for Establishing Cemeteries around the Metropolis*.[29] There is a wonderful denunciation of Norwood: 'The condition of this Cemetery is the most deeply degrading of all. We have read the tax clauses of the Bill with utter astonishment . . . they are monstrous beyond credibility. It is enacted by Clause XVIII

[137]

that upon every corpse removed for interment in this Cemetery from any parish in the County of Surrey, or from Lambeth, or Battersea, or Wandsworth, or London, or Westminster, or Southwark, a tax of *twenty shillings* shall be paid, if buried in a vault, or catacomb, or brick grave, and of seven shillings and six pence, if buried in the open ground, to the incumbent of the parish whence it was brought! We really thought that, in Bishop Blomfield's Ten Shillings Model Cemetery at Westminster the climax of extortion had been reached; but here the enormous impost is doubled; and we have it on good authority, that, but for the indignant resolve of a certain Lay Lord, the Bishops would have added some eight shillings more! How heathenish, my Lord of London, must be the soil of Norwood!

It is profane, imperfect, (oh, too bad!)
Except—and bishoped by thee!'

The pamphlet suggested that the cemetery companies were in cahoots with the City and that the gravediggers' evidence was 'cooked'. On p 47, *The Horrors of Enon Chapel Examined*, we are informed that Mr Mackinnon had it all his own way, but on examination, many of the witnesses were of doubtful value. 'Mr. Walker and his associates . . . have indulged in . . . misrepresentation, delusion, and slander.' The records of Mr Howse of Enon Chapel show that the interments were one quarter of what the witnesses alleged. Mr George Alfred Walker was denounced as being 'credulous and imaginative', carrying everything to excess. 'Extravagance of thought and of diction' marked his evidence throughout, according to the pamphlet. The Bishop of London was quoted as saying he had known hundreds of lead coffins in vaults none of which was in a poor state. 'Whom will you believe', Mr Edwards asked; 'the quiet Bishop, or the effervescent Apothecary?'

It is clear that Dissenters were keen on keeping their own

burial grounds, however insanitary. What they objected to was, in fact, giving money to the Established Church. Since some of the most offensive burial places were Nonconformist burial grounds and vaults, such as Spa Fields, Enon Chapel, and others, we must draw the conclusion that the problems of the overcrowded burial grounds were almost purely financial in origin.

So it might have continued had not a singular calamity struck the cities of Britain. The growing population in ever more built-up cities only faced the fact that the churchyards were full up and could not cope when the cholera struck. The ignorance of the populace and the professions in the face of the epidemic is staggering. As late as 1854 Charlton Lane, incumbent of the parishes of Kennington, Stockwell, and South Lambeth, produced a pamphlet for his parishioners, *How to Meet the Cholera*, which included several unlikely causes of cholera and how to deal with it.[30] The medical profession declared that cucumbers, fogs, 'feverish vapours', and other improbable culprits were responsible for cholera. Public opinion was outraged, and new standards were demanded for sanitary reform. As early as 1832 posters appeared in London which asked:

Has

D E A T H

(in a rage)

Been invited by the Commissioners of Common Sewers to take up his abode in Lambeth? Or, from what other villainous cause proceeds the frightful Mortality by which we are surrounded?

In this Pest-House of the Metropolis, and disgrace to the Nation, the main thoroughfares are still without

Common Sewers, although the Inhabitants have paid exorbitant Rates from time immemorial!!!

'O Heaven! that such companions thou'dst unfold,

'And put in every honest hand, a whip,

'To lash the rascals naked through the world.'

Unless something be speedily done to allay the growing discontent of the people, retributive justice in her salutary Vengeance will commence her operations with the *Lamp-Iron* and the *Halter*.

SALUS POPULI

Lambeth, August, 1832.

J. W. PEEL, Printer, 9, New Cut, Lambeth.

When, however, the cholera epidemics reached plague proportions, it was the last straw, and the legislation was duly passed which indicated that parliament now considered that the interment of the dead was an unfit subject for commercial speculation. In 1850 an Act of Parliament constituted a Metropolitan Burial District and granted the General Board of Health power to provide burial grounds and to purchase the commercial cemeteries which had already been established.[31] The Board of Health proposed to transform Kensal Green into the Great Western Cemetery, and also proposed a Great Eastern Cemetery, which *The Observer* calculated would be at Erith. Receiving houses were proposed for the banks of the river. When we realise that in 1850 a gentleman's funeral cost £100 and an artisan's cost £5 in the Joint Stock Company Cemeteries, the case for radical reform is demonstrated.[32]

Unfortunately the Treasury was not very co-operative with the idea of forming 'a distant Metropolitan Cemetery, or rather Necropolis, upon a grand and comprehensive scale ... equally called for by health, by economy, and by decency'. The board considered the existing cemeteries quite unsuitable in terms of subsoil (which was usually a stiff clay); of layout; of design; and of building. By 1851 the Egyptian, Greek and fanciful cardboard Gothic of the 1830s was quite unfashionable, and so even the chapels were considered inappropriate. As a result, the board intended to close the existing cemeteries as soon as the large new ones were formed. There was also the question of position, for as the city grew, so the cemeteries would have to be established further away.[33]

Brompton and Nunhead were the first two cemeteries to be considered, and, as we have seen, only Brompton was acquired. Today, there is a striking contrast between the cemetery in the hands of what is now the Ministry of Public Building and Works and the derelict overgrown cemetery in private hands.

More Cemeteries. Funerals by Railway

There appear to have been three main schemes proposed in 1850 to satisfy the demand for cemeteries. These were the London Clergy Plan; the Board of Health and Erith Plan; and the Woking Necropolis Plan,[34] which was based on the idea of setting up one huge necropolis for the whole of the country, run by the State, and linked to the towns by water and by the railways. The Great Eastern Cemetery, or Erith Plan, had the backing of the Commissioners of the Board of Health, including Edwin Chadwick, who pointed out that the existing cemeteries failed to cater for the poor. The river would have been the main route of conveyance, and 'reception houses' for corpses would have been erected at various points. This fell through, but the Woking idea was realised, although not as a state concern, but as a private company, the political climate in Britain not then being amenable to state enterprise or to a non-profitmaking enterprise. It is interesting to compare the British attitudes of the 1850s with those of New York in the late 1830s, mentioned in Chapter 9.

The London Necropolis & National Mausoleum at Woking originally bought 2,000 acres. It was a private company, incorporated in July 1852. It was opened in 1854. *The Times* of 14 February 1855 reported on the affairs of the London Necropolis Company in detail, and how, with the graveyards closing down in large numbers, the company would do well. The cemetery was opened on 13 November 1854. Arrangements were made with the parishes of St Luke's, Chelsea, Bermondsey, and Chiswick. The directors were in touch with the parochial authorities of St Leonard's, Shoreditch; St George the Martyr, Queen Square; St John's and St Margaret's Westminster; St George the Martyr, Southwark; St George-in-the-East; The Whitechapel Union; and Deptford. Roman Catholics were to be catered for, as were Jews. The great innovation, however, was that the London Necropolis and National Mausoleum Company came to an arrangement with the directors of the London and South Western Railway whereby funerals would *go by train* to Woking. The result was a station by Tite in London, and a design for one in Woking by S. Smirke, who was architect to the company. Tite also advised on the general layout. Naturally, the expense of an arrangement run for profit left the dead of the poor uncatered for. Only when public cemeteries were formed was the problem overcome.

A visit to Brookwood Cemetery today is saddening. The Southern Railway station is still there and functioning, but the two stations (one for Dissenters, Roman Catholics, Parsees, and others, and the other for Anglicans) are deserted, for no track runs to them now. Smirke's splendid Gothic station was never built (page 143), and cheap structures of wood and cast iron were erected. The line of the railway track is still (1970) visible, but the connection with

S. Smirke's design for a Gothic station at Brookwood Cemetery

the metropolis seems to be breaking. Monuments stand over
the mass graves of those who were once buried in crypts
and graveyards in Southwark, Shoreditch, and Bloomsbury.
However, the planting, largely evergreen, and with vast
American trees and rhododendrons, is imaginative, and the
effect is magnificent. Considering labour costs, the cemetery

is still well cared for. The chapels are of dull design and the lodges are of no interest. Clearly hygiene was of first consideration in this, the largest of all the London cemeteries. A large military cemetery for several nations has been established there, with monuments by Sir Edward Maufe and others. There are a few distinguished tombs, including the charming Italian Romanesque family tomb (page 145).

Brookwood is very open, very airy, very spacious, and is still a profit-making private company. The first crematorium was established near there, at St John's, in 1878, with apparatus designed by Gorini, but the structure was crude and functional. A more sophisticated building was erected in 1889, to designs by E. F. Clarke.

The new legislation changed the scale and the system. A few more private cemeteries were formed after 1850, notably the Woking Cemetery in Surrey, properly called Brookwood; the East London Cemetery of thirty acres founded by the East London Cemetery Company, Grange Road, Plaistow, in 1872; and the Great Northern Cemetery at Colney Hatch in 1861. This last cemetery was founded by the Great Northern Cemetery Company Ltd, and was originally planned to cover nearly two hundred acres. The plan was a series of concentric avenues around a central point occupied by the Anglican chapel, a well-proportioned building in the Gothic taste. The chapel was originally planned with catacombs under, but only a few of these were built. The inside of the chapel was unfortunately adapted as a crematorium in the 1950s, and the strong Victorian interior has been altered beyond recognition. The spire is a fine sight through the trees, however, and the excellent planting of the cemetery, so obviously influenced by Loudon, is still in good condition, despite the inevitable undergrowth which has developed since the war. The architect for the Great Northern Cemetery was Alexander Spurr, who died on 25 November

'The charming Italian Romanesque family tomb in Brookwood Cemetery'

1872 and is buried near the chapel. The surveyor was Morris Evans, of 7 John Street, Adelphi. The Great Northern Cemetery has a number of communal graves for the former occupiers of crypts and vaults in the City. Of particular interest, however, is the collection of individually labelled vault slabs under which are re-interred the distinguished dead from the Savoy Chapel in the Strand, mostly Hanoverian courtiers and persons of distinction from even earlier times. This cemetery was also designed to be served by a branch of the Great Northern Railway, and a signal box still bears the word 'Cemetery' as a reminder. Of the station, practically nothing remains although the Company still operates.

Most cemeteries were run by public bodies after 1850.

7 The City of London Cemetery Paddington Cemetery, and others laid out by public bodies

That grounded maxim
So rife and celebrated in the mouths
Of wisest men; that to the public good
Private respects must yield.

John Milton: Samson Agonistes

THE CLIMATE OF OPINION thus brought about government action in the encouragement of public cemeteries, and we have seen that the Metropolitan Interments Act caused some consternation among the boards of the earlier, smaller, metropolitan cemeteries. The Woking Necropolis Plan, published as part of *Extramural Burial. The Three Schemes*[1] was the major private-enterprise cemetery to be established after the compromise solution which permitted both private speculation and public bodies to operate cemeteries.

Under the Act of Parliament of 1852 when the Vestries were empowered to establish Burial Boards several public cemeteries were formed. *The Builder* of 3 December 1853 tells us that the foundation stone of the church for the new cemetery at Finchley for St Pancras was laid by the vicar of that parish. This was, in fact, the first of the new cemeteries, and comprised some eighty-six acres. The architects were Barnett and Birch, and a dreary job they made of it. Apart from early troubles with the drainage which caused much of the ground to be waterlogged, the architecture is undistinguished, and the quality of the recent addition of a crematorium has not helped.

Two cemeteries from this period stand out as being of really fine design, however. The first of these was the Paddington Cemetery, and here the implementary powers of the original Burial Act are expressed. Once more Père-la-Chaise was the model, and a planned system of burial is evident (page 148). The influence of Loudon is apparent in the planting, and in Paddington we no longer find the Portland stone painted with preservative which was so common in other cemeteries: instead there is a wealth of granite, pink, grey, and green, imported from Aberdeen, Peterhead, and Stonehaven, which towns did a steady trade in Rubislaw, Corrennie, Kemnay, and Blackhill granites shipped to the Port of London.[2] This robust material

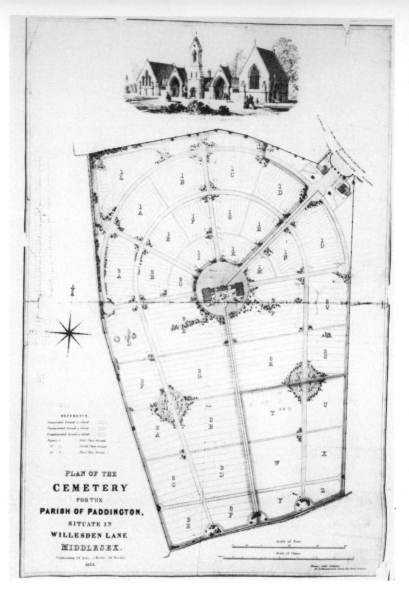

Plan of Paddington Cemetery, by Thomas Little

declined in favour in the 1890s and Carrara and Sicily marbles were imported instead to create those bleak, glaring wildernesses of repellent angels and obnoxious cherubs that disfigure so many of our urban burial grounds today.

[*148*]

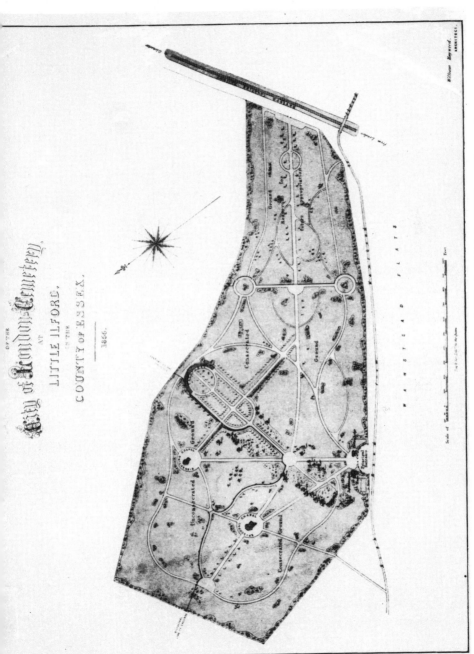

Plan of the City of London Cemetery at Little Ilford, 1856, by William Haywood

Paddington Cemetery was designed by Thomas Little, who also designed much of Nunhead. The chapels are part of the one complex, linked by two *portes-cochères* with a belfry in the centre of the composition. The cemetery appears to be among his last works, for he died three years after it was opened. The chapels are designed in utilitarian Gothic, but the black woodwork, of massive section, is impressive enough, and the whole is of a simplicity which is hard not to admire (page 148).

Of much greater importance than Paddington, however, is the grand and splendid City of London Cemetery at Little Ilford, opened on 24 June 1856. This was an attempt to alleviate the pressures caused by the closure of so many City churchyards, and the plans were published in 1856. This cemetery was formed under the direction of the Commissioners of Sewers of the City of London from the designs and under the direction of William Haywood.[3]

The site was chosen six miles from the 'City Boundary at Aldgate, that being the nearest point at which, by the Clauses of the Metropolitan Burials Act, 15 and 16 Vict. c 85, a Cemetery at the Eastern end of the Metropolis could be formed'.

Access was via Bow and Stratford to the Great Essex Road. The site was originally the Earl of Mornington's property, and 'is bounded on the North by the Wellesley Park Estate; on the South, by the Eastern Counties Railway. The soil is of a fine bright gravel.'[4]

The total area was originally 89½ acres, of which 49 were consecrated, 21 acres were for Dissenters, and 19½ were unappropriated. Works of draining and enclosing started in June 1854. All buildings except the catacombs were finished in 1855 for Christmas.[5]

The architect for this cemetery of Augustan calm and Olympian scale was William Haywood (page 149). Born on

Haywood's tomb at Little Ilford

8 December 1821, he was a pupil of George Aitchison, RA. He became assistant surveyor to the Commissioners of Sewers for London in 1845, and was chief engineer from 1846 until his death. He worked closely with the celebrated Joseph Bazalgette, whose Abbey Mills pumping-station is still, despite much mutilation, one of the grandest sights in London.

Dissenters' chapel at Little Ilford

Haywood will be remembered for two magnificent works: Holborn Viaduct (designed with details by James Bunstone Bunning) and the City of London Cemetery. He died at 56 Hamilton Terrace, Maida Hill, on 13 April 1894, and was cremated at St John's, Woking. His ashes, however, repose in his tomb at Little Ilford (page 151).[6]

The site at Little Ilford, as the district was then called,

covered 200 acres. It was originally the site of the Manor of Aldersbrook, but the Manor House had long since vanished by the time Haywood laid out the cemetery. By the purchase of the ground certain commoners' rights over Wanstead Flats and Epping Forest were acquired. This enabled the Corporation to sue the parties who had wrongfully possessed themselves of forest land, and so, eventually, Epping Forest was preserved for the recreation of Londoners.

The cemetery now covers about 130 acres, with about 40 in reserve. The influence of Loudon is immediately apparent, for the beauty of the trees, rhododendrons, and azaleas echoes his praises of the Arboretum at Abney Park and indeed reminds us of his own treatise on the subject.[7] The excellent standard of maintenance is an indictment of certain companies and authorities who have let their cemeteries decay almost beyond redemption.

The plan is ingenious. Curving roads wind through the cemetery, meeting at *rond-points*, at two of which the chapels are situated. The catacomb valley is formally planned near the eastern boundary wall (page 154).

The site of the former Aldersbrook Lake, famed for carp, roach, and perch, is now occupied by the Catacomb Valley, a charming place surrounded by rhododendrons, chestnuts, and limes. Haywood resisted the idea of building catacombs, but was overruled, and we may be thankful that he was, for the long, low line of masonry contributes greatly to the qualities of the landscaping (page 154).

The cemetery has several enclosures in which lie the remains of those people formerly buried in City churchyards and crypts which had been closed and cleared. The most notable monuments are those to the many dead of St Mary Aldermanbury and of St Mary Somerset.

The chapels are in a spiky Gothic (page 152), and the crematorium, dating from Edwardian times, is also Gothic,

[*153*]

The Catacomb Valley, City of London Cemetery

with a highly unconvincing tower disguising the flues. The lodge is idiosyncratic, but pleasing nevertheless.

This brings us to a fundamental point in the consideration of Victorian cemeteries: their connection with style. Only a quarter of a century lies between Kensal Green and the City of London Cemetery or Brookwood. Yet the difference in style and in scale is immense. It is possible to walk the few acres of the earlier cemeteries and to get a sense of enclosure, of romantic feeling, and of a plethora of detail from Egyptian to Greek, and from Roman to Gothic.

Oddly enough, it is not from Geary, Bunning, Haywood, Little, Griffith, Baud, or any other architect that we obtain an explanation of this strange eclecticism which is more apparent in cemeteries of the Victorian age than in the townscape. It is John Claudius Loudon who sheds light on

[154]

the problem, and enables us to see the small-scale macabre charm of Highgate as very much part of the same movement which was to end by producing Brookwood and Little Ilford.

Loudon's theory of architecture was strongly moral, as might be expected of a Scot, and an early nineteenth-century Scot at that. Loudon exalted the taste of the common man, and demanded social reform, wholesale education, and improvement of minds. Loudon, like Archibald Alison, held a philosophy of what might be termed common sense, and that, in the context of art, beauty was in the eye of the beholder who determines whether something is acceptable or not. To Loudon, and to men like him, the purpose of education was to give to the minds of men, all men, as many potential associations as possible, so that the purpose of the artist was to strike an answering chord in the educated man by creating an association in his mind. Alison himself wrote that, if we saw an object, it might be beautiful to us, but that, if we knew it was the residence of any person whose memory we admire, 'a train of associations comes to mind'. 'The delight with which we recollect the traces of their lives, blends itself insensibly with the emotions which the scenery excites; and the admiration which these recollections afford, seems to give a *kind of sanctity*[8] to the place where they dwelt, and converts everything into beauty which appears to have been connected with them.'[9]

It is clear that the germ of this philosophy of 'associations' with the dead was the core of much nineteenth-century cemetery layout *and* tomb design. Loudon himself, who, as we have seen, was involved directly or indirectly with most of the London cemeteries, had what might be described as a functional basis for all his criticism. This is especially apparent in *On the laying out, planting, and managing of Cemeteries; and on the Improvement of Churchyards, with sixty engravings,* published in 1843, and in his more famous *Encyclopaedia of Cottage, Farm and Villa Architecture*.[10]

Loudon clearly felt that, in architecture, problems of beauty, proportion, or scale were not visual ones, but were functional in essence. Is the building fit for its purpose? Quite obviously, Loudon's opinions on most of the cemetery designs of his day were not high, with the exception of Brandon's gate-lodge at Tower Hamlets, and the Arboretum of Abney Park.

The Victorian cemeteries, which for so long have been avoided by many commentators as objects for serious study for the reason that they offer too great a puzzle to those who aspire to punditry on Victorian architecture, give us the key to the Victorian approach. The literal meanings behind what might at first appear to be a confusion of styles were aspects of a search for truth. The tumultuous detail of Victorian cemeteries and the use of historical ornament were not only highly educational, but were almost whimsical at times. The Victorians did things in a big way, and their cemeteries echo that grandeur of vision and hope for a future which vanished in 1914. Styles, for Loudon, were ephemeral, but had temporary functions in that they could awaken untutored minds to a sense of history. As universal education progressed, so, to Loudon, the necessity for 'styles' as such would cease to be important. His illustrations in the *Encyclopaedia* show his versatility in everything from Cardboard Gothic to Indian Nash; but his insistence on fitness for function anticipates the twentieth century.

It must not be forgotten that the cemeteries were originally formed in response to the functional need to dispose of the dead of the growing metropolis, and gradually the ornamental nature of Brompton and Highgate gave way to the huge and almost rural cemeteries at Little Ilford and Brookwood. The latter might be seen as the culmination of

[*156*]

Loudon's ideas, for the buildings are bare, but dignified, and the planting recalls his ideas for Norwood. The use of the railway as an up-to-date means of conveyance for corpses from the metropolis would have appealed to him.

According to a parliamentary return issued in the 1870s the number of churchyards in England and Wales then open was 9,989, while the number closed was 843. The closing of churchyards proceeded very slowly, even though in 1854-5, after the Burial Acts had been passed, as many as 541 consecrated burial grounds were closed.

It was from the 1860s onwards that many cemeteries were established, not by private enterprise, but by public bodies. The new, non-denominational cemeteries were hygienic, and the reformers who had agitated for their establishment could regard their victory with some satisfaction. However, the extremists pursued public health to the lengths where it was proposed to deny royalty the right to be buried in the vaults at Windsor.

The later cemeteries tend to be dull, dreary places, and there can be few sights as melancholy as the huge, barren wastes of white marble with hardly a tree or a shrub to soften the visual harshness. Landscaping tends to be of the most apologetic kind, and there is nothing of the pleasant Arcadian planting of Ilford, Abney Park, or Highgate.

As open-air sculpture galleries and schools for instruction in architecture, landscape gardening, arboriculture, and botany, the new cemeteries were hailed with enthusiasm. William Robinson, obviously much influenced by Loudon, was an advocate of landscaped garden cemeteries, with trees and tasteful monuments, and he supported cremation and urn burial as being more likely to provide the conditions for agreeable landscape design.[11]

The huge cemeteries of Britain established simply as a means of disposing of corpses are a sad contrast with the charm and romantic qualities of the early Victorian cemeteries. The London cemeteries and those of Glasgow and Liverpool mentioned in this book are undoubtedly the finest and most interesting from the landscaping and architectural points of view. There were others of remarkably fine quality, at Newcastle-upon-Tyne, for example, where the architect Dobson designed many monuments as well as lodges and other buildings; and many cities in Britain acquired cemeteries of pleasant character. The majority of cemeteries founded in mid-Victorian times are dull, ugly, and uninteresting, however, and the mass-produced white marble tombstones are excruciating compared with the splendours of early monumental design. The marvellous inventive genius displayed in Sir John Soane's own monument in the churchyard of St Giles-in-the-Fields, for example, is a rebuke to those standardised monuments of late Victorian, Edwardian, and modern times.

There can be few ways of wasting money in order to blight the landscape more pathetic than the erection of hideous tombstones. Apart from the harshness and the ugliness, they are a sad commentary on how far monumental design has sunk since the times of those noble memorials.

The reformers were therefore getting their way, but at the expense of aesthetic considerations. The new public cemeteries were hygienic, but they were also lacking completely in taste, elegance, charm, or architectural quality, with a few exceptions already mentioned.

It was a curious reversal of history when, despite the reforms, conditions were still appalling in several areas, not in the churchyards of the Anglican communion this time, but in private burial grounds. One of the worst of these was at Victoria Park in Bethnal Green, London. It was owned by the Butler family, and was established in 1845 by C. S. Butler, a member for the Tower Hamlets, who failed to win a seat when a candidate for the new borough of Hackney because he raised the burial fees at the ground on Sundays. In 1876 about 200 bodies per week were buried in this small eleven-acre cemetery. Most of the graves were common, and apparently about 300,000 bodies had been crammed into the space. In some of the East End parishes efforts had been made to form public burial grounds, but these had been 'defeated by a joint combination of Radicalism and Dissent'.[12] Victoria Park Cemetery was laid out by the Metropolitan Public Gardens Association in 1894, and is now known as Meath Gardens.

Many burial grounds were closed by Orders in Council, and under the Disused Burial Grounds Act, 1884,[13] the Metropolitan Board of Works (Various Powers) Act, 1885,[14] and the Open Spaces Act, 1887,[15] provision was made for the future use of such burial grounds, including their conversion into public gardens.

With the growth of cemeteries and the victory of the reformers it became apparent that cemeteries became rapidly filled and used a considerable amount of land. Once, bodies had been crammed into small areas, and so graveyards did not impinge too much on the visual scene. When bodies were buried in single graves, however, and regulations controlled exhumation and the management of cemeteries, land was rapidly used, and cemeteries became huge, utilitarian, and ugly. To counteract this, Francis Seymour Haden wrote a pamphlet in which he proposed a solution. He observed that the evils which the cremationists held to be inseparable from the principle of interment were wholly the fault of burial custom. He attacked the unreasoning sentiment which prompted people to bury their dead in such a way that the earth could not have access to the corpses, and suggested that legislation should be enacted to ensure the body's dissolution by the earth. A body enclosed in an air-tight coffin putrefies, and may be found years afterwards in a state of advanced but unprogressive decay. If, however, it is exposed to the earth, it breaks down quickly, and takes on the qualities of earth. Haden proposed a new kind of coffin which would not prevent dissolution. It would be very thin, or the top and sides could be removed after the body had been lowered into the grave, or it could be of wicker or lattice work, open at the top and filled with fragrant herbs. Models of these wicker coffins were exhibited at Stafford House, and aroused much public interest. Haden also suggested that bodies could be embedded in charcoal in a crypt to which the air had free access for a year, after which time the bones could be stored in catacombs or buried. He suggested that all the cavalcade and accessories of funerals could be abolished, the body being conveyed by rail or water to the cemetery, the mourners and friends assembling in the chapel. Two thousand acres would bury the dead for ever, since the ground could always be reused.

The London Necropolis Company actually developed 'Earth to Earth' coffins. These conventionally shaped coffins had the advantage of being closed but, when buried, they very quickly disintegrated, allowing the body to be resolved into its constituent elements. The gravelly soil of Brookwood was ideally suited to 'Earth to Earth' coffins, and the progressive company lost no time advertising their new coffins, which could be inspected at their offices.

The excellent and sensible ideas of Haden did not receive acceptance on anything like the scale they merited. The undertaking trade had much to lose if the expensive funerals described in Chapter 1 went out of fashion. There was another lobby, however, which was to prove much more successful in getting its ideas accepted. The cremationists had appeared on the scene with a vengeance.

8 The rise of cremation

Einst, o Wunder! entblüht auf meinem Grabe
Eine Blume der Asche meines Herzens;
Deutlich schimmert auf jedem Purpurblättchen:
Adelaide!

Friedrich von Matthissohn (1761-1831)

It is not my intention to give a complete history of the cremation movement. That has been adequately covered elsewhere. I shall look at the cremation movement in relation to the cemeteries. In an article by H. C. Delves on 'The Disposal of the Dead'[1] the problem is summed up by the various methods used. Bodies may be 'interred, exposed, cremated, preserved, artificially decomposed, buried in water, devoured by wild animals or birds, eaten in token or complete cannibalism'. The 'cemetery', we are reminded, is derived from the Greek, meaning a 'sleeping place'.

A survey by the Cremation Society in 1951 showed that municipal burial space covered more than 25,000 acres in England and Wales. Churchyards and private cemeteries accounted for approximately double that figure. About 0.13 per cent of the land surface was used for burial. An annual increase of 400 acres was forecast per annum. Yet, as Arnold Whittick wrote, the cemeteries have provided much needed open spaces which have helped to break up the unrelieved sprawl of buildings.[2]

One of the earliest cremations in modern times seems to have been of the body of Honoretta Pratt, who died in September 1769. The event was recorded in the old churchyard of St George, Hanover Square. That worthy woman, believing that the vapours arising from the graves in the churchyards of populous cities might prove harmful to the inhabitants, and resolving to extend to future times, as far as she was able, that charity and benevolence which distinguished her in life, ordered that the body should be burnt, in the hope that others would follow her example; a thing too hastily censured by those who did not inquire into her motives.

In Dorset in 1882 Lady Hanham and her daughter-in-law were cremated in a small furnace constructed especially for the purpose. No doubt classical history had played its part in drawing attention to the possibilities of cremation. Sir Thomas Browne had published *Hydriotaphia, Urne Buriall*,[3] and the *Origin of Cremation* by J. Jamieson had come out in the *Proceedings of the Royal Society* published in Edinburgh.[4] In 1822 the drowned Williams and Shelley were both cremated on a beach in Italy. It is supposed by many that this method of disposal was chosen as a dramatic ending to a romantic career, while some have thought Byron to be responsible as an *enfant terrible* of the period. The facts are very different, for there was no option in the matter, Italian law requiring anything washed up from the sea to be burnt on the shore. This, of course, was a precaution against the introduction of disease. A military guard was dispatched, and a grid of iron was supplied by the authorities, under which were piled logs from the pinewoods near by. An officer of health supervised the arrangements. Frankincense, salt, wine, and oil were thrown onto the burning pyre, and eventually the body was reduced to a skeleton, which was buried in the Protestant cemetery in Rome. The inefficient cremation left the heart untouched, and this was plucked from the flames. Leigh Hunt witnessed the whole ghastly business from Byron's carriage, while Byron, unable to stand the sickening smell, left before it was over. He begged the others to ensure that his own body was not burnt. 'Let my carcase rot where it falls', he said.

W. Eassie's *Cremation* was published in 1875,[5] and *Cremation considered in reference to the Resurrection* by 'A Truth-Seeker' appeared in London in 1874.[6] The latter quotes cases where cremation is expressly demanded in times of pestilence.[7] 'A Truth-Seeker' produced a most reasoned pamphlet, and pointed out the absurdities of 'Christian' arguments against cremation. The Jews burnt their dead when it was absolutely necessary, not only in times of plague, but to prevent indignities being done by enemies.

[*163*]

'All the valiant men arose, and went all night, and took the body of Saul and the bodies of his sons from the wall of Bethshan, and come to Jabesh, and burnt them there. And they took their bones, and buried them under a tree at Jabesh, and fasted seven days.'[8]

Sir Henry Thompson advocated cremation in the *Contemporary Review* of January 1874, and in the same year Bishop Fraser, when opening Bolton Cemetery, drew attention to the beliefs of the ancients and pointed out the fact that the dissipation of buried bodies was considerable.[9]

In 1876 a congress was held in Dresden. Extraordinary designs by Carl Pieper and Gustav Lilienthal of Dresden were exhibited showing a grandiose crematorium and mortuary buildings using the Siemens Regenerative Process, contrived by Friedrich Siemens. *The Transactions of the Cremation Society of England* 1877-1912 gives a full account of the movement. Included is a description of the cremation of the Chevalier Keller in 1876 in Milan.[10] Another account of this was published by the Keller family.[11] This crematory was in the form of a sarcophagus under a large open temple. A small flame of coal gas was visible at the top of the urn, as a symbol that the work was proceeding. Eventually, Keller's crematory was abandoned. The gas-holder behind was removed, and in 1880 suitable wings were added and more up-to-date apparatus was installed.

In 1884 Mr Justice Stephen in R v *Price*, declared that it was not an offence to burn a body provided that no nuisance was caused. In 1875 the Council of the Cremation Society had decided to establish a crematorium, and in 1878 a site was selected at St John's, Woking, with apparatus designed by Professor Gorini. Cremation was legally sanctioned in 1885, and the first subject at Woking was a woman. The initial design was utilitarian, and was mostly chimney. The actual crematorium buildings in red-brick

Siemens's cremation apparatus (from The Last Act, *by William Tegg. London, 1876)*

Gothic with stone dressings were designed and built in 1889 to designs by E. F. Clarke.

One of the most interesting schemes for cremation apparatus is that of Messrs Siemens, which consists of a gas-holder, a furnace with a regulator and a space for burning, and a chimney. The cremation process is carried out by gas conducted through a pipe provided with a regulating valve, where, meeting with air, it burns fiercely. The flame extends through the chamber so that the brick lining is made white-hot. The covering of the chamber is removed, the coffin is lowered into position (page 165), and the cover is replaced. The picture of this apparatus in action is interesting because it shows the cleric and mourners as though round a grave, the coffin being lowered into the furnace.

Sir Henry Thompson continued his untiring campaigns, and in a pamphlet entitled *Cremation in Great Britain*,[12] it was pointed out that concentrations of people need crematoria. All cremations are now carried out under an Act of Parliament passed in 1902 with subsequent revisions. Section 10 of the Births and Deaths Registration Act 1926[13] also applies.

The early crematoria are fairly successful architecturally, especially Sir Ernest George's Golders Green Crematorium of Edwardian times, but a decline in design as the Celebration of Death has waned has produced a large number of poorly designed, undignified, and in some cases positively scruffy buildings.

Since crematoria are now in use all over the country, it is astounding that their functional and liturgical bases have not been subjected to closer scrutiny. Now that the Roman Catholic Church has taken the decision to permit Catholics to be cremated, it appears that there will be a fairly widespread swing towards almost universal cremation practice.

[*166*]

It is a sobering thought that, generally speaking, crematoria in this country fail dismally in the provision of appropriate surroundings to the solemn occasions of funerals.

Historically, the cremation movement was a secular one, and religious trappings have been grafted on later. The uncomfortable and unresolved design of crematoria appears to stem from this basic difficulty, although other factors, such as a desire to protect relatives from the facts of cremation, contribute to the distressing pseudo-gentility of many crematoria.

Cremation appealed to the Victorians because of its highly practical nature in the improvement of the hygienic disposal of the dead. There was some religious opposition because of the belief in bodily resurrection, but, Sir Henry Thompson pointed out, cremation is not incompatible with religious rites, but enables them to be conducted with ease and comfort. (This argument ignores the fact that cremation was strictly forbidden by the early Christian Church.) The process also destroys infection, and prevents any injury to the living, but then a coffin buried six feet deep is also quite harmless.

Ashes may be buried, scattered, or stored in urns or caskets in columbaria. There were several Victorian schemes for building huge pyramids[14] in which ashes could be stored, and for building cremated remains into walls specially constructed for the purpose. The columbaria provided in early crematoria contained niches which could be purchased for a fixed period or for perpetuity. These columbaria were probably the last instance where anything approaching dignity was applied to the design of buildings associated with the Celebration of Death.

In terms of robust sureness of design the Victorians have much to teach us when it comes to providing a fit setting for the disposal of the dead.

[*167*]

9 Cemeteries and Funeral Customs in the United States of America and elsewhere

But see! the well-plum'd herse comes nodding on,
Stately and slow; and properly attended
By the whole sable tribe, that painful watch
The sick man's door, and live upon the dead,
By letting out their persons by the hour,
To mimic sorrow, when the heart's not sad.
How rich the trappings, now they're all unfurl'd,
And glittering in the sun! triumphant entries
Of conquerors, and coronation-pomps,
In glory scarce exceed. Great gluts of people
Retard th'unwieldy show: whilst from the casements
And houses' tops, ranks behind ranks close wedg'd
Hang bellying o'er. But! tell us, why this waste?
Why, this ado in earthing up a carcass
That's fall'n into disgrace, and in the nostril
Smells horrible? Ye undertakers! tell us,
Midst all the gorgeous figures you exhibit,
Why is the principal conceal'd, for which
You make this mighty stir? 'Tis wisely done:
What would offend the eye in a good picture,
The painter casts discreetly into shades.

Robert Blair: The Grave

NINETEENTH-CENTURY FUNERAL customs across Europe and America were basically similar. The English landscape traditions were universally acceptable for cemetery design, except in the cities of the south and among the Jewish communities. Italian and South American cemeteries tend to be very urban in character, due to the density of burial and the size of the monuments, while Jewish cemeteries tend not be be landscaped because of the possibility that the roots of trees would disturb the bodies.

Most nineteenth-century cities in Europe and America ran into similar troubles as those experienced in England, and large cemeteries were founded in order to alleviate the problems caused by intramural and churchyard interment. French cemeteries tend to be much more formal than those in England, with the exception of Père-la-Chaise, which influenced English cemetery design and was itself originally inspired by romantic English landscape traditions. In France, there are many tombs of iron and glass, which give a somewhat horticultural character to the provincial cemeteries.

Italian cemeteries were very grand. Genoa's Staglieno, designed by Carlo Baralino in 1835, consists of a square surrounded by colonnades. The square is paved with marble, tombs underneath. The big square has since been crossed by more arcades containing monuments. Rising above, to one side, is a cliff with cypress-bordered ramps and a grand stair that lead up to a terrace where the tombs of the rich are situated. A circular 'Pantheon' covers a room for the coffins of the newly dead. This cemetery, realised by the architect Grasso, from Baralino's drawings, contains the graves of Mazzini and of members of the Risorgimento. A crematorium is also provided.

The concept of a paved square surrounded by colonnades is ancient, the most celebrated example being undoubtedly the Campo Santo at Pisa, built between 1278 and 1283 to designs by Giovanni Pisano. The beautiful open tracery around the cloisters was added in 1463. Other cemeteries based on this plan exist in many cities, notably Salzburg and New Orleans.

In the United States of America, burial places were at first individual plots on farms or near the houses of settlers. Where villages or towns had churches, interment took place in the churchyards. As in Europe, these churchyards became overcrowded and insanitary, and it became necessary to form cemeteries outside the towns. Mount Auburn in Boston was the first (1832), and Philadelphia and Green-Wood in New York soon followed.

It is interesting to note that when the Green-Wood Cemetery was first proposed, it was, like the British ones, to be operated by a Joint Stock Company, capital being raised by shares of 100 dollars each giving a total of $300,000. However, the company idea was thought to be unsavoury, and trustees were appointed by the Legislature of the State of New York, the body corporate being chartered by an Act of the Legislature on 18 April 1838. Funds were raised by giving bonds, pledging the proceeds of the undertaking in lieu of cash as payment for the land. Thus no profits or gains would accrue to any individual.

The site of the Green-Wood Cemetery was very hilly and leafy, and was large, comprising some 200 acres. The idea behind the name was the antithesis of the Necropolis as found in New Orleans, Glasgow, or Liverpool. Green-Wood Cemetery might be described as the first Garden City of the Dead. Before 1839 the dead of New York suffered similar indignities to those of the dead of British cities. With a population of 300,000 in 1839, New York was often forced to bury its dead in the new cemeteries of Mount Auburn in Boston or Laurel Hill in Philadelphia.

The new cemetery was divided into 300sq ft lots, each

with a margin of one foot all round. The lots sold for $100 each.[1] Green-Wood became one of the richest of American cemeteries, the Père-la-Chaise or Kensal Green of New York, and was a popular place to visit in the late nineteenth century,[2] fares from Fifth Avenue being 25 cents. Drivers showed and explained all the monuments of interest as well as the principal parts of the cemetery, this service being run by the cemetery authorities.

The most famous cemetery in the United States, apart from Forest Lawn Memorial-Park, is the Arlington National Cemetery. This is a large cemetery, four hundred acres in area, and is situated in Virginia, on the banks of the River Potomac, opposite Washington DC. It was founded in 1864 when the grounds of the Custis-Lee mansion became a military cemetery by order of the secretary of war. The United States government obtained a clear title to the site in 1883, by the payment of $150,000 to George Washington Custis Lee. Many famous Americans, including L'Enfant the designer of Washington, Pershing the general, W. H. Taft, J. F. Kennedy, and Robert E. Peary, are buried in this noble cemetery, which is attractively sited and landscaped, and very well maintained. Cannons, blockhouses, obelisks, pyramids, piled arms, prisms, and other objects enliven its appearance. Many cemeteries founded during the Civil War are imaginatively laid out and pleasantly planted.

The romantic nineteenth-century tradition that created Père-la-Chaise, Kensal Green, Highgate, Mount Auburn, Green-Wood, and, to a lesser extent, Arlington National Cemetery, has given way to a new concept. The term 'cemetery' is now in some danger of extinction in the United States, for the euphemism 'Memorial-Park' is in vogue. These 'Memorial-Parks', where graves are marked by flat metal plates, appear to be superseding the nineteenth-century model cemeteries. They are based on the Forest

Lawn Memorial-Park, immortalised by Evelyn Waugh and Jessica Mitford.[3] Gentility, euphemism, comfortable suburban death, and banality are replacing the splendours of nineteenth-century cemetery design.

Forest Lawn has concert halls, chapels, a cinema, and many other items far removed from the realities of death. It was founded by Hubert Eaton at the end of World War I, and was originally an older cemetery that had gone to seed. Eaton made it respectable and created a tourist attraction into the bargain.[4]

America adopted European notions in the nineteenth century, but in the twentieth, it seems that the process is being reversed. There are signs that the 'Memorial-Park' concept is gaining acceptance in Europe. Clearly, the ease of maintenance and the absence of tall memorials has a certain attraction for the tidy-minded, but the qualities of the nineteenth-century cemeteries should not be overlooked. There are advocates of the 'Lawn' principle who suggest that all monuments should be removed, but it is to be hoped that their iconoclastic zeal will not prevail.

It was not only cemetery design that the United States emulated. The first general mourning proclaimed there was on the death of Benjamin Franklin in 1791, and the next was when Washington died. The obsequies of President Lincoln, however, were on a much more elaborate scale, and the funeral journey to Springfield lasted twelve days. The railway carriage that carried the coffin was completely draped in black, the mourning outside being festooned in two rows above and below the windows. The engine was covered in crape, and it carried draped flags. At several points *en route*, a halt was made, and the coffin was removed from the train so that funeral services might be held. The body was buried at Oak Ridge Cemetery, Springfield, on 3 May 1865. During the period between the President's

[*172*]

death and his interment, every city and town in the Republic testified to the greatest grief, and public expressions of mourning were universal. New York presented a striking appearance. There was scarcely a building not draped in deepest mourning, and long festoons of black and white muslin drooped everywhere. Show-cases outside shops were dressed with funeral rosettes.

Scarcely less magnificent were the obsequies accorded to the whisky-drinking General Grant. Funeral services were observed in towns and cities of every state and territory of the Union, amid a display of mourning-emblems of great lavishness. New York was again extravagantly draped. The procession route was nine miles long, and it is estimated that three million people saw the funeral, in which over 50,000 persons joined, including 30,000 soldiers. The head of the procession arrived at the grave three and a half hours before the funeral car, which was drawn by twenty-four black horses, each one led by a black attendant, and each covered with sable trappings.

Perhaps it would be appropriate at this point to consider the significance of various colours for mourning in different parts of the world. Black expresses the privation of light and joy, the midnight gloom for the loss sustained. It is and was the mourning colour in Europe, America, ancient Greece, and Rome. Black and white stripes express sorrow and hope, as in the case of Lincoln's funeral, and are the mourning colours of many South Sea Islanders.

Greyish brown is the colour of the earth to which the dead must return. It is the colour of mourning in Ethiopia. Pale brown, on the other hand, is the colour of withered leaves, and is the colour of mourning in Persia.

Light blue expresses the hope in heaven, and is the colour favoured by Armenians, Syrians and Cappadocians. Deep blue has a sinister meaning for the carpet-makers of

Turkestan, while the ancient Romans wore the colour to signify mourning. Purple and violet are the colours of mourning for royalty, and for princes of the Church.

White is the colour of mourning in China. Women in ancient Rome and in Sparta sometimes wore white mourning, and it was also the colour of grief in Spain until 1498. In England and the United States it was customary in country districts to wear white silk hat-bands when mourning the unmarried and the very young. Queen Victoria had a 'white' funeral, oddly enough.

Yellow is the colour of mourning in Burmah and other far eastern countries, and was also so in Egypt and Brittany. Scarlet was worn by Louis XI of France, and was occasionally regarded as a mourning colour in the Middle Ages.

If the American Way of Death, so delightfully yet horrifically described by Jessica Mitford, has been accepted up until now, there are signs of change. In Britain, funerals are generally very simple, and cremation is on the increase. While many members of the 'dismal trade' could wish for American customs to become acceptable in Britain, there is possibly some evidence that more simplified funerals are being desired by more people in America. After all:

> Sepulchral columns wrestle but in vain
> With all-subduing Time: his cank'ring hand
> With calm delib'rate malice wasteth them:
> Worn on the edge of days, the brass consumes,
> The busto moulders, and the deep-cut marble,
> Unsteady to the steel, gives up its charge.
> Ambition! half convicted of her folly,
> Hangs down the head, and reddens at the tale.[5]

The expensive 'caskets' purveyed by American undertakers do nothing to prevent the inevitable decay of the body. Even 'embalming' is superficial, and serves to delay putrefaction long enough for the corpse to be displayed in an open coffin in a 'funeral parlour'. Full embalming, in the sense that the body of Lenin is embalmed, is rare, and pointless unless some political or religious purpose is intended. If a head of state is to have a funeral several weeks after death, and the body is to be exposed, then clearly some preserving process should be employed, and some cosmetics should be applied. There can be little excuse, however, for what Jessica Mitford describes as the treatment given to 'poor old Oscar' with a heavy 'sun-tan' and the 'wrong shade of lipstick' as the normal run of things.

The denial of death which euphemisms, cosmetics, 'caskets', 'Memorial-Parks' and the like imply, is evidence of a peculiar state of affairs. Very different is the last word in this chapter which I give to H. A. Driver, and which sums up the truth:

It was a mausoleum, vast and high,
Whose soil was reeking with mortality:
There, in the midst, O sight of horror! stood
Three forms whose aspect chilled my vital blood:
Grouped on a grave's cold slab, like things that breathed,
Three skeletons their fleshless arms enwreathed;
But moveless—silent as the ponderous stone
Whereon they stood:— and I was all alone!
"O for the Ethiop's sable charms to hide
Those hideous vestiges of Beauty's pride!"
To this I heard a hollow voice reply,
"Behold the GRACES!— mortal, feast thine eye!"
But I did turn me, sickening with disgust;
For I beheld them mouldering into dust.[6]

10 **Conclusion**

Oh, let me range the gloomy aisles alone:
Sad luxury! to vulgar minds unknown:
Along the walls where sparkling marbles show
What worthies form the hallowed world below.
Thomas Tickell, On the Death of Addison

The Dangers of Premature Interment

Many aspects of death fascinated the Victorians. As early as Loudon's book on cemeteries a room had been set aside at the cemetery of Frankfurt-am-Main for corpses.[1] Strings were attached to the fingers of the corpses, and these were attached to bells. It was forbidden to inter a body until infallible signs of decomposition were obvious. When Lord Lytton died, he directed that his body should not be coffined, disturbed, or moved from his bed until three medical men had declared in writing that signs of decomposition had unmistakably commenced.

It was the poetess Friederike Kempner who was responsible for the widespread use of mortuary chambers in Germany, because of Kaiser Wilhelm I's interest in her book on premature burial.[2] Hallam quotes a limerick current at the time:

> There was a young man at Nunhead
> Who awoke in his coffin of lead;
>   'It is cosy enough',
>   He remarked, in a huff,
> 'But I wasn't aware I was dead'

in *The Burial Reformer*.[3] The magazine changed its name to *Perils of Premature Burial* shortly afterwards, and remained under Hallam's editorship. The magazine ceased publication in 1914. It has, of course, been very common practice in the North of Ireland among Protestants to sever arteries after death to ensure that premature burial does not take place. Removal of the heart or a post-mortem dissection would accomplish the same ends.

Recent cases of persons found alive in morgues after being certified dead should revive Miss Kempner's idea of waiting-rooms where bodies can wait until they decay. Certainly refrigeration as practised now is the opposite of what should be provided.

Concern over the problems of premature burial was very real. Diagnosis was so poor that frequently 'bodies' revived. There was a real hazard that premature burial could take place. In *Projet pour prévenir les Dangers Très-Fréquens des INHUMATIONS précipitées* by le comte Léopold de Berchtold[4] it was suggested that the only safeguard was to wait until manifest signs of corruption were evident.

The cudgels for burial reform were taken up by the redoubtable Arthur Hallam. *The Burial Reformer*, a quarterly journal, was edited by him, the first number coming out in 1905. Many cases of revival after 'death' were recorded. The Accrington sensation of 16 January 1905 was told in some detail. Apparently a Mrs Holden, aged twenty-nine, was laid out as dead, and the task was almost completed when the undertaker was startled to notice a slight movement. He revived her, and she survived.

It is on record that, when Frank Buckland was deputed by the College of Surgeons to seek John Hunter's body in St Martin-in-the-Fields, he opened several coffins, and found at least three where premature burial had obviously taken place. Sir Benjamin Ward Richardson, an early cremationist, said that the only trustworthy sign of death was 'distinct decomposition'. Dr Franz Hartmann of Florence had the same views. George Berkeley, Bishop of Colne (1685-1753), directed that his body be kept above ground for five days after death. Daniel O'Connell said: 'Do not bury me until I am dead.'

In the April 1906 issue of *The Burial Reformer*[5] there is an interesting article by Albert C. Freeman on Waiting Mortuaries for the prevention of premature burial. Other attempts were made to get over the problem, notably by Count Karnice-Karnicki's apparatus, which consisted of a 3½in tube, a sealed box, and a ball which lay on the chest of the corpse. Any movement operated a signal above the

[*178*]

ground and sprang a door, which admitted light and air into the coffin.

'Death, Heaven, and the Victorians'

From 6 May to 3 August 1970 a singular exhibition was held in the Brighton Art Gallery & Museum, Sussex, entitled 'Death, Heaven, and the Victorians'. To visit it was a revelation of what Dickens described as the 'fat atmosphere of funerals', and the emotions were profound, varying from astonishment to melancholy, and from embarrassed amusement to a desperate enthusiasm.

Of the London cemeteries, the exhibition brochure[6] said that 'with their tangled undergrowth, large trees and gaping grandiloquent tombs—contemporaries complained of the lack of foundations[7]—broken columns, urns, sarcophagi, temples, are today powerfully evocative of the transitory nature of life. They have acquired a romantic melancholy that should be preserved.'

The Victorian age was one of faith and doubt. Conflicting sects vied with each other and produced their own individual architectural expressions. With the discoveries of Charles Darwin, however, faith was rocked to its foundations, and the Victorians were racked by doubts and searchings. At the same time, many accepted the literalness of the Victorian heaven, peopled as it was with angels, cherubs, and other wonderful creatures.

The Victorian age seems to be far from us today, almost beyond recall. Nowhere is the strangeness of the period, with its obsessions about death, its high moral tone, and its sentimentality, better expressed than in the cemeteries, yet nowhere is the practicality of the Victorians better indicated. Today heaven, and especially the Victorian heaven, is beyond our grasp, yet death is every man's lot. It is all the more astonishing to reflect that there are many Victorians still living today, yet our attitude to death has changed utterly. Gone are the splendid funerals which even I can remember as a child, with black horses, carriages, top hats, feathers, and magnificence. Coffins today are cheap-looking, where once they were beautifully polished, with splendid handles and plates. Do we compose thundering articles for the public prints concerning the morally uplifting influences of cemeteries? Do we suggest that cemeteries are useful for 'instruction in architecture, sculpture, landscape gardening, arboriculture, botany, and in those parts of general gardening, neatness, order and high keeping', as Loudon once wrote?

The cemeteries are in danger, for we no longer understand them. They have passed into the realms of the fabulous, and, as such, are embarrassing to our society because they actually exist.

We can scarcely comprehend the problems of the age, when a major bone of contention was the payment of a fee to the incumbents of parishes from which the corpses had come. Pamphlets such as *The Burials Question Further Examined From a Layman's Point of View. Is there a Grievance?*[8] discuss the question of Nonconformists being buried in the parish churchyards of the Church of England. *On Burial, Death and Resurrection*[9] touches on general theological problems.

Fearsome arguments over the appropriateness of certain tomb designs were published. Pugin argued for the use of the cross as a grave monument, and this was accepted, despite the fact that it had been considered to savour of Popery hitherto. Memorial brasses came back into fashion, and Gothic became the most respectable style for tombs.

Several books of suitable designs were published, among them *A Manual for the Study of the Sepulchral Slabs and Crosses of the Middle Ages*, by the Rev Edward L. Cutts.[10]

[*180*]

Victorian dress could, by judicious arrangement, appear to be medieval, especially for clerics and ladies, so effigies came back into fashion. Cardinal Wiseman's monument, which used to stand in St Mary's Cemetery, Kensal Green, but was transferred to Westminster Cathedral later, is a case in point. It is a canopied tomb by E. Welby Pugin, and a sketch design drawing of it by C. A. Buckler (1824-1905) exists in the Drawings Collection of the Royal Institute of British Architects. Various eminent architects designed tombs, including Geary, Bunning, Baud, Little, Pugin, Street, Allom, R. C. Hussey, J. F. Bentley, A. J. Humbert, and C. Miles.[11] [12]

Humbert's design for the royal mausoleum at Frogmore was spectacular, although the superb interior was by Professor Ludwig Gruner from Dresden, obviously a follower of Semper.[13] Lord Leighton made designs for Mrs Browning's tomb in Florence, and Alfred Stevens designed several monuments, including that of the Duke of Wellington, in St Paul's. An incredible design for a mausoleum exists at Madame Tussaud's in model form. It is made of paper from old memorial cards and mounts, and was fashioned by Charles Peace, the celebrated murderer, to while away the time before his execution. Peace apparently had an ambition to have a large mausoleum, and spent whatever time he had left over from his career as a burglar in designing the most gorgeous one possible, to be finished in marble and gold. Needless to say, his ambition was never realised, for he was hanged for murder in 1879, and the authorities did not see fit to cause his monument to be erected over his remains.

Summary
We have seen, then, how the state of the churchyards in the eighteenth century worsened in the nineteenth with the

growth of population in the expanding metropolis. Chaos resulted in emergencies, such as the cholera epidemics. Agitation for reform got under way. There had been similar agitation in the seventeenth century when many proposed cemeteries outside the City. The plague made this proposal even more attractive.

There was a certain amount of opposition from the churches because of loss of revenue as well as a feeling for the religious significance of the burial of the dead in or near churches. Contemporary descriptions by Carden, Walker, and others show the conditions in the City churchyards to have been vile. Coffins were frequently smashed up and burned or reused. Iron coffins were introduced to foil the body-snatchers, the grave-diggers, and sextons (who were sometimes in league with the Resurrectionists), but of course iron coffins do not decay, so they were quickly prohibited. Some eccentrics advocated cremation. Shelley's cremation caught the imagination, but, despite proposals, orthodoxy was horrified, and punishments were threatened.

Cholera epidemics created such a problem that even the most hard-boiled opposition had to give in. At first the cemeteries were small, well-planted, and endowed with architecture, and were operated by joint-stock companies. Principles were laid down for proper disposal of the dead, without sentiment, and as a purely functional answer, like drains or water supply. Plans were drawn up so that plots were accurately determined, and bodies were buried deep enough to avoid the scandals of the City churchyards.

The nineteenth-century cemeteries, besides having the functional *raison d'être*, were thought of as being morally uplifting, educational, and instructive. They were considered to be amenities, and their value as open spaces in the fully built-up urban matrix is of enormous importance. They reflected the tastes and aspirations of a society.

[182]

Splendid Classical tombs are gradually superseded by Gothic, then back to Classical again. The treatment of the catacombs, mausolea, chapels, planting, lodges, and layout was highly original and very much of the nineteenth century. There is humour, banality, sentiment, power, profundity, and sheer vulgarity in the individual tombs.

Since Victorian times cremation has been accepted. From early beginnings, there are pressures today to make cremation compulsory. Labour costs and other problems have contributed to the decline of the upkeep of the cemeteries. The companies never were an enormous success financially, and the establishment of local-authority cemeteries hastened their decline. Attempts to get over the pleasing chaos of the Victorian cemetery by introducing the 'lawn' system have only destroyed the character. Grave-yards are becoming as suburbanly smooth as Croydon or Surbiton. Some aspects of Victorian robustness still survive, however, in the East End cemeteries, where families go on a Saturday to see Grandad, whose photograph may frequently be placed on the tombstone. The standard of design of modern headstones is, however, abysmally low.

The value of the nineteenth-century cemeteries today as open spaces in the metropolis is enormous. The trees are now mature; the graves and monuments have taken on the patina of age, and often, as in Highgate, an Arcadian quality exists which would be ruined by a conversion to a pure park. Some cemeteries are dreary, however, and have none of the qualities of Ilford, Highgate, or Kensal Green. Tower Hamlets Cemetery and others are being gradually cleared, and they will be converted to parks. This may be successful, but there is a strong case for preserving the most interesting tombs, sculpture, or lettering, and a photo-graphic record of the lesser monuments should be made. The marvellous tomb of Sir John Soane in the old cemetery

Sir John Soane's tomb in the burial ground of St Giles-in-the-Fields at St Pancras

of St Giles-in-the-Fields is a case in point, for here is a really splendid and highly original work of architecture in characteristic Soane style (above). How unfortunate it looks, however, set among the trim lawns and roses! There is also a case for preserving some cemeteries just as they are, and the establishment of a repair fund for the best of the architecture and sculptures, chapels, and mausolea.

Shaw, Wells, and others were enthusiastic cremationists. At present, the cremation ceremony is an anticlimax. A curtain drawn over, or a coffin moving alone through a door or down a hatch, lacks the drama of a coffin going down into the earth or into a fiery furnace. This is a comment on our society, where death is played down and made apparently insignificant, like suburban life. If cremation becomes universal, then it should be carried out with the conviction and *panache* that the Victorians brought to their cemetery designs. The first crematoria, built by Victorians, allowed the mourners to see the coffin disappear into the fire. Since World War I we have become too genteel for such an acceptance of the functional aspects of body disposal.

The fundamental function of a crematorium is to dispose of bodies. It must have other functions as well, however, for religious rites may be celebrated, and in most cases there will be friends or relatives present who are, in fact, symbolically taking leave of a social personality. Ceremony is a factor in the disposal of the dead throughout all history, and the rites involve actions, words, music, and movements which add up to a pattern forming the framework within which feelings are expressed. The fulfilment of mourning or the taking leave of a friend is dependent upon this framework. Unfortunately most crematoria have no recognisable form, and their purpose is lost in a welter of crude and pompous design. 'Their form does not derive from considerations of the liturgy, which is not surprising since there is no rite for cremation' wrote P. B. Bond in an excellent article in *The Architectural Review*.[14] 'It is simply the burial service, clumsily adapted and inappropriately used for the purpose. Yet for a great number of people cremation is a religious act, and it would be reasonable to expect the guiding principle in the arrangement of those parts of the building used in a religious service to be the liturgical expression of a religious rite.'

In practice, however, persons arrive at a building of indifferent, mediocre, or even bad design, into which they go with no ceremony and a great deal of emotional discomfort. The coffin may already be on the catafalque or it may be carried in. A minister may conduct a somewhat abrupt service, or friends may read poetry or prose. At the words of committal several varieties of scheme are in operation. In some crematoria a curtain is drawn, so that the coffin is no longer in view. In others, it is lowered through the floor. In some cases the coffin moves horizontally through a wall via a door or a tawdry curtain. In all these cases the service is now over, so the mourners disperse, with the uncomfortable knowledge that the coffin has disappeared, but they have not *seen* any obvious finale. The coffin passes to a committal chamber where it is placed on a trolley. It is then conducted to the furnace at once or it may wait. Of course, two relatives or friends may actually witness the placing of the coffin in the furnace, but this is an optional extra and not part of the ceremony. The committal spoken of in the service is not a committal at the time. The committal should be the climax of the ceremony and the point at which the farewell is made. As Mr Bond wrote, 'it is the reality of the end of earthly life as we know it. This moment can only be expressed by a true and direct committal at the time and not, as at present, by merely removing the coffin from view . . .' In earth burial, the significance of the lowering of a coffin into a grave is profound, and those who witness it have a deep emotional experience which becomes part of their lives. The reality of death has been faced, and the severing of a link has been suffered. No such significance is apparent in the cremation ceremony.

[*186*]

Naturally, the disposal of ashes provides a problem. It is not generally realised that, when cremation has finished, the remains are still recognisable as being the bones of a human being. The ashes are cooled and then ground up in a pulveriser.[15] Nails from the coffin are removed, and what finally emerges in a casket is a fine ground grey-white powder which may be preserved in an urn or scattered. Some ashes are preserved in columbaria; others are buried; others are scattered.[16] Most crematoria possess rose-gardens which are memorials to the dead.[17] These rose-gardens have an air of depressing gentility, far removed from the robust drama of the great nineteenth-century cemeteries. The regimented lines of roses outside the crematorium, with no variation, no visual drama, no contrast, are a sorry answer to the wonderful landscapes superb architecture, exciting vistas, and varied tombs of the Victorian Celebration of Death.

We are left with crumbling buildings, overgrown grave-yards; some wonderful places, others completely run down. What are we to do? As stated before, the cemeteries are assets in a city short of open spaces. In east London some of the cemeteries function as open spaces for recreation although burials continue. We must conserve the open spaces, without destroying the best of the qualities of the places. Cemeteries are history and they are a repository of the history of taste. The Victorians were functionalists in the disposal of their dead.

Often headstones in churchyards or cemeteries are removed or piled up against a wall on various pretexts such as those of 'unsightliness', 'untidiness', 'difficulty of keeping the weeds at bay', and so on. I dispute the theory that stones provide a bad setting for a church. I argue against the removal of any of the monuments, inside or outside, because I believe that they are a record of what people and

[187]

craftsmen have felt about one of the great and significant human experiences. Those feelings have been expressed in design, in lettering, in choice of words, in size, and in materials, so that monumental stones are documents of changing tastes.

The reminders of death, inside and outside a church, or in the cemeteries of the first half of Victoria's reign, convey an ever present visual memorial to our collective past. Jeremy Bentham advised that one's ancestors should be embalmed and kept around the house and gardens, and although his suggestion has practical difficulties, he certainly grasps the point that without a connection with our ancestral past we become loose and unsettled, and drift, with no roots and no tribal memory. The obliteration of cemeteries and church-yard memorials reflects the unease with which society views death, seeking to keep it out of sight and out of mind. Of course, there are problems with labour, and clearly neglect must not be allowed to produce an overgrown wilderness. But the current obsession with keeping every-thing tidy, not accepting long grass and leaning tombs, and treating a funeral as a refuse disposal problem, reflects a deep malaise in society. Death was never a tidy thing: it is foolish to try to make it so, and to compartment it away from life and the living.

The cemeteries founded in the nineteenth century were answers to a functional requirement. They produced a rich and varied number of solutions to the problems posed, and gave architects, gardeners, sculptors, and engineers great scope. They are pointers to the tastes and aspirations of society; Classical first; then Gothic and then back to simpler forms; and finally debased and vulgar.

There is pathos to be found in the Victorian cemeteries. When we read of all the Willies, Georges, Charlies, Marys, and Vickys who died in infancy, 'too good for the world', or because 'the angels wanted him' or 'her', we can begin to understand the daily sorrows of the average Victorian family. We read the pompous eulogies with a faint amusement or perhaps distaste, and wonder who could have deserved such ponderous prose. We see names and dates and addresses and ages all recorded, and we wonder what the people were like and how they sounded and looked. We imagine their daily lives, and wonder what struck down Emma, dear wife of Frederick, in her twenty-third year. Then we consider the neglect, the overgrown state of many of the cemeteries, the decaying tombs, and we wonder what has become of the families. Have they all died, or been dispersed, or gone abroad, or do they simply not care? I suspect not caring is part of the problem, perhaps the major one, and a Stepney epitaph recognised this with the sad, cynical, but humorous verse:

> My wife she's dead, and here she lies,
> There's nobody laughs, and nobody cries;
> Where she's gone, and how she fares,
> Nobody knows, and nobody cares.

Cemeteries are cruel and cold and frightening at dusk, and few would wish to linger as a thin mist rises from the rank grass and the undergrowth, threading its way through the gravestones. In winter, when even the softening effects of foliage have been lost, the trees rise up in agony, it seems, from a myriad of bent and leaning tombstones. Few can wish to be there, alive or dead, at such a time, and the glories of the chapel architecture or of the sculpture or planting probably pass most people by.

Yet when the flowers appear, when the trees become green again, and a warm sun dries the withered leaves about the graves, cemeteries can become lyrically beautiful and utterly charming. A spring morning in Tower Hamlets

[*189*]

Cemetery can bring so much loveliness into the place that many will stroll there rather than in the Mile End Road or the municipal open spaces; May morning in Abney Park reveals the beauty of an astonishingly varied planting that would grace any botanic garden; while a summer afternoon in Highgate becomes a memory as poignant as a visit to some peaceful Italian garden where sculpture and planting create a vividly full impression.

Who could forget the stately Greek Revival of Kensal Green (page 72)? Who would deny the theatrical power of the Egyptian Revival at Highgate (page 94) or the gates of Abney Park? Who could ignore the strange, melancholy Gothic of Nunhead, and the inverted torches symbolising death on the entrance gates? Who would fail to respond to the spacious dignity of the City of London Cemetery at Ilford when the rhododendrons are in bloom, and the smell of new-cut grass is heavy in the warm air? Who could forget the imagery of the Glasgow Necropolis, or the deep, black classicism of Liverpool? Who could deny the majesty of Norwood (page 80) or the weird power in the deserted colonnades at Kensal Green?

The neglect of cemeteries and the contemporary playing down of death (page 191), are, in my opinion, symptomatic of how society collectively wills it. The underprivileged of today can be found among our own people: they are the old and the infirm, those already halfway or more to death. Old age, like death, is a taboo subject. Even death is being robbed of its profound significance as a part of life in the half-world and semi-darkness of our present society. Death is the supreme achievement and the end of a cycle; it is a rounding off and a finale. Today, the dignity which should be given and accorded to those who grow old or those who die has been reduced to considerations of giving the minimum physical comforts to those no longer

[*190*]

The neglected cemetery

economically productive, and of disposing of the refuse once life is extinct. This deprivation of man's dignity is a source of sober reflection, and is expressed in the institutionalised hospital wards, old people's homes, municipal burial grounds, and incinerators of the dead.

The Victorian legacy of housing, transportation, sewers, water supply, and reforms of all description has been discussed amply in recent years. The Victorian contribution in the field of disposal of the dead has been overlooked. It is time we assessed their achievements in this as in other ways. They apprehended the problems with gusto and realism—a realism which we should be well advised to study as lessons for our own half-hearted approach to the Celebration of Death.

Bibliography

CHAPTER 1

1 Haweis, Rev H. R. *Ashes to Ashes. A Cremation Prelude* (1875)

2 Puckle, Bertram S. *Funeral Customs. Their Origin and Development* (1926), 97

3 Ibid 98

4 Davey, Richard. *A History of Mourning* published at Jay's, Regent Street, W (*c* 1890)

5 Ibid

6 Puckle 107

7 Ibid 112

8 *In Memoriam, or, Funeral Records of Liverpool Celebrities* (Liverpool 1876). This gives details of furnishings, funerals, and ceremonial

9 Briggs, Asa. *Victorian Cities* (Harmondsworth 1968), 59

10 For further information concerning Literary influences on the Gothic Revival see Clark, Kenneth. *The Gothic Revival* (Harmondsworth 1964), 17-33

11 Quoted in Clarke, Basil F. L. *Church Builders of the Nineteenth Century* (1938, reprinted Newton Abbot 1969), 11

12 This theme is further developed in Curl, James Stevens. *European Cities and Society. The Influence of Political Climate on Town Design* (1970)

CHAPTER 2

1 Curl, James Stevens. 'Highgate: a great Victorian cemetery', *The Journal of the Royal Institute of British Architects* (April 1968)

2 Knight, Charles, ed, *London*, vol 5 (1841-4 with later editions), 163

3 Puckle, 44

[4] Pope, Alexander. *Moral Essays*, Epistle 1 (1733)

[5] Evelyn, John. *Diary*

[6] Taylor, Joseph. *The Danger of Premature Interment Proved from Many Remarkable instances of People who have recovered after being laid out for dead and of others entombed alive for want of being properly examined prior to Interment* (1816), 98

[7] Evelyn, John. *Diary*

[8] Stow, John, Citizen of London. *A Survey of London Contayning the Originall, Antiquity, Increase, Moderne Estate, and Description of That Citie, written in the year 1598* (1603)

[9] Curl, James Stevens. 'Highgate'

[10] *The Builder* (1843), 175

[11] Ibid

[12] Ibid 104

[13] Timbs, John. *Curiosities of London* (1885), 75

[14] Light, Alfred W. *Bunhill Fields* (1913), 2-3

[15] Curll, Edmund. *The Inscriptions upon the Tombs, Grave-Stones, &c. in the Dissenters Burial Place near Bunhill-Fields* (1717)

[16] *Proceedings in Reference to the Preservation of Bunhill Fields Burial ground with Inscriptions on the Tombs* (1867)

[17] Holmes, Mrs Basil. *The London Burial Grounds. Notes on their History from the Earliest Times to the Present Day* (1896)

[18] Lewis, Reverend Thomas. *Seasonable Considerations on the Indecent and Dangerous Custom of BURYING in Churches and Churchyards, with remarkable OBSERVATIONS historical and philosophical. Proving that the Custom is not only contrary to the Practice of the Antients, but fatal, in case of INFECTION* (1721)

[19] Ibid

[20] Webb's *Collection of Epitaphs* (1775)

[21] Dickens, Charles. *The Uncommercial Traveller*. Various editions

[22] Dickens, Charles. *Bleak House*. Various editions

[23] Genesis, chapter 23, verse 17

[24] Normand fils. *Monumens Funéraires Choisis Dans les Cimetières de Paris et des Principales Villes de France* (Paris 1832)

[25] Marty. *Les Principaux Monuments Funéraires Du Père-Lachaise, de Montmartre, du Mont-Parnasse et autres Cimetières de Paris Dessinés et Mesurés par Rousseau, architecte, et Lithographiés par Lassalle, Accompagnés d'une Description succincte du monument et d'une Notice historique sur le personnage qu'il renferme* (Paris 1840)

[26] Godwin, William. *An Essay on Sepulchres, or, a proposal for erecting some memorial of the illustrious dead in all ages on the spot where their remains have been interred* (1809)

[27] *In Memoriam, or, Funeral Records of Liverpool Celebrities* (Liverpool 1876)

[28] *The Morning Chronicle*, Thursday, 10 June 1830

[29] Strang, John. *Necropolis Glasguensis with Osbervations* [sic] *on ANCIENT AND MODERN TOMBS and SEPULTURE* (Glasgow 1831), 48-55

[30] *The Gardener's Magazine*, vol 18 (1842), 51

[31] *The Gardener's Magazine*, vol 19 (1843)

[32] Loudon, J. C. *On the laying out, planting, and managing of Cemeteries; and on the improvement of Churchyards with sixty engravings* (1843)

[33] Knight, Charles, ed *London*, vol 4 (1841-4 with later editions), 170

[34] Laughlin, C. J. 'Cemeteries of New Orleans', *The Architectural Review*, vol 103, no 614 (February 1948)

[35] Miller, Thomas. *Picturesque Sketches of London Past and Present* (1852)

[36] The 'sweet breathing-places' are especially valuable today, now that the cities have expanded so much

[37] Miller, 274-5

CHAPTER 3

1 *Gentleman's Magazine*, 1830, vol 100, pt i, 552

2 Ibid 351

3 Ibid 1832, vol 102, pt ii, 171

4 Kendall, H. E., architect, *Sketches of the Approved Designs of a Chapel and Gateway Entrances intended to be erected at Kensall Green for the General Cemetery Company* (1832)

5 *The Builder*, 9 January 1875, Kendall's obituary

6 Ibid

7 *Gentleman's Magazine*, 1832, vol 102, pt ii, 245

8 p 108

9 Pevsner, in *London, except the Cities of London and Westminster, The Buildings of England Series* (Harmondsworth 1952), attributes the designs of the chapels to Paul, but he was probably working from the misleading *Builder* obituary of Paul

10 *Gentleman's Magazine*, 1833, vol 103, pt i, 169

11 Ibid, 1832, vol 102, pt ii, 17 and 245

12 J., W. *Illustrated Guide to Kensal Green Cemetery* (c 1858)

13 Walford, Edward. *Old and New London* (1887)

14 *The Mirror of Literature, Amusement and Instruction*, Saturday, 28 April 1838

15 Ibid, Saturday, 18 November 1843

16 Mss collection in the Kensington and Chelsea Public Library, Local History Collection

17 Geary, Stephen, architect. Founder of the Cemeteries at Highgate, Nunhead, Peckham, Westminster, Gravesend, Brighton, etc. *Cemetery Designs for Tombs and Cenotaphs* (1840). This book contains twenty-one designs of remarkable coarseness engraved by B. Winkles.

18 *The Builder*, 27 December 1856, 700

19 Ibid, 2 September 1854, 460

20 Trendall, E. W., architect. *A New Work on Monuments,*

Cenotaphs, Tombs and Tablets, etc. etc. with their details drawn to a large scale, by which the Workman can erect each design with facility (c 1840). 30 plates

21 Bunning, J. B., architect. *Designs for Tombs and Monuments* (1839). This is a series of designs some of which have great delicacy of feeling

22 Edward Blore published *The Monumental Remains of Noble and Eminent Persons, comprising The Sepulchral Antiquities of Great Britain* in London in 1826

23 For general and particular information here I am much indebted to the General Cemetery Company, and especially to Mr Malyon. This company had offices at 95 Great Russell Street, Bloomsbury, but now operates from the lodge itself on the Harrow Road. Much of the information contained within is from the minutes of the General Cemetery Company, now in the offices at Harrow Road

CHAPTER 4

1 Walford, Edward. *Old and New London* (1887) vol 5, 220

2 *The Times*

3 Strang, John. *Necropolis Glasguensis*

4 *Annales de Chimie*, vol 5, 154; Walker, G. A. *Gatherings from Graveyards*, 86; and an article on 'Adipocere' in Ure's *Dictionary of Chemistry*. See also Stephens. 'Incidents of Travel', *The Saturday Magazine*, vol 20, 141. See also *The Gardener's Magazine*, vols 18 and 19

5 Strang, John. *Necropolis Glasguensis*

6 Loudon, J. C. *On the laying out, planting and managing of Cemeteries; and on the improvement of Churchyards, with sixty engravings* (1843)

7 *The Builder*, vol 1 (1843), 51

8 The South Metropolitan Cemetery Company had offices at 13 New Bridge Street, London, EC

9 6 and 7 William IV, c 129, local

10 Wilson, J. B. *The Story of Norwood*. Unpublished
11 *The Architectural Review*, vol 147, no 876, for February 1970
12 *The Survey of London*, vol 26, *The Parish of St Mary, Lambeth*. Part Two, Southern Area (1956)
13 Boase, Frederic. *Modern English Biography containing many thousand concise memoirs of persons who have died between the years 1851-1900* (1965)
14 Cansick, Frederick Teague. *A Collection of Curious and Interesting Epitaphs, copied from the existing monuments of Distinguished and Noted Characters in the Cemeteries and Churchyards of Saint Pancras, Middlesex* (1872)
15 Lloyd, John H. *The History, Topography and Antiquities of Highgate, in the County of Middlesex* (1888), 494-95
16 Curl, James Stevens. 'Highgate'
17 Prickett, Frederick. *The History and Antiquities of Highgate* (1842), 80
18 Ibid, 83
19 Lloyd, 494-95
20 Timbs, John. *Curiosities of London* (1885), 82
21 Justyne, William. *Guide to Highgate Cemetery* (*c* 1865)
22 *The Mirror of Literature, Amusement and Instruction*, no 912 for Saturday, 15 Sept 1838
23 *The Literary World; a journal of popular information and entertainment conducted by John Timbs, eleven years editor of The Mirror*, no 17, Saturday, 20 July 1839
24 Lloyd, 494-5
25 In the Local History Collection of the Camden Library
26 Boase
27 *The Builder*, obituary of J. B. Bunning
28 *The Croydon Weekly Standard*, 25 November 1865
29 *The Builder*, 18 May 1878, 513
30 *The Times*, various dates
31 Lloyd, 495

[32] See *Hansard*, vol 313, no 35

[33] *The Times*

[34] Whittick, Arnold. 'Planning and Cemeteries', *Town and Country Planning*, February 1952, 81-6

[35] *The Builder*, vol 17 (1859), 855

[36] Ibid, 17 August 1861, 560

[37] Ibid, vol 3 (1845), 179

[38] These bills are now in the Record Room at County Hall in London

[39] *The Hampstead and Highgate Express* (1970)

[40] For further information see *The Rules, Orders and Regulations of the London Cemetery Company*, 7 February 1878

As a matter of interest, a chamber in the Lebanon Circle, fitted, complete with shelves for fifteen coffins, was priced from 200 gns (Highgate)

A chamber in the Avenue catacombs, fitted for 12 coffins, cost 130 gns (Highgate)

A place in the Chapel catacombs cost 15 gns, ie for one coffin (Nunhead), and a common grave was 2 gns (Nunhead)

CHAPTER 5

[1] 1 Vict, c 130, local. *An Act for establishing a Cemetery for the Interment of the Dead Westward of the Metropolis by a Company to be 'The West of London and Westminster Cemetery Company'*

[2] Stephen Geary is described as the 'Founder of the Cemeteries at Highgate, Nunhead, Peckham, Westminster, Gravesend, Brighton, etc.' in the *Cemetery Designs for Tombs and Cenotaphs*, published in London in 1840

[3] Minutes of the West of London and Westminster Cemetery Company, now in the Public Record Office. PRO Works 6/65, 2-35

[4] Minutes, 39-44

[5] Ibid, 70
[6] Obituary in *The Builder*, vol 33 (1875), 402
[7] Minutes, 71-94
[8] Ibid, 211
[9] By 1841 these were already going out of favour
[10] Minutes, 243
[11] Ibid, 470
[12] 10 and 11 Vict c 65, public
[13] 13 and 14 Vict c 52, public
[14] 15 and 16 Vict c 85, public
[15] *The Builder*, 22 December 1866, 938
[16] See the preceding chapter

CHAPTER 6

[1] *A Supplementary Report to her Majesty's Secretary of State for the Home Department from the Poor Law Commissioners on the Results of a Special Inquiry into the Practice of Interment in Towns,* 1843, written by Sir Edwin Chadwick, of Poor Law Reform fame
[2] *The Builder*, vol 3 (1845), 588
[3] Ibid, 53
[4] Ibid, 69
[5] Ibid, 82
[6] Ibid, 92
[7] Ibid, 110
[8] Ibid, 157
[9] Ibid, 173
[10] Ibid, 178
[11] Knight, vol 4 (1841-4, with later editions), 163
[12] Ibid
[13] Ibid, 164
[14] Curl, James Stevens. 'Highgate'
[15] Knight
[16] *The Builder*, vol 3 (1845), 197

[17] Ibid

[18] Ibid, 310

[19] Ibid, 518

[20] Ibid, 525

[21] Ibid, vol 4 (1846), 571

[22] Ibid, 586

[23] Ibid, 281

[24] Ibid, 395

[25] Ibid, vol 5 (1847), 139

[26] Ibid, 424

[27] Wilson and Levy. *Burial Reform and Financial Costs* (1938)

[28] Anon. *The Cemetery. A Brief appeal to the feelings of Society on Behalf of Extra Mural Burial* (1848)

[29] Edwards, James, *et al. Health of Towns. An examination of the Report and Evidence of the Select Committee; of Mr. Mac-Kinnon's* [sic] *Bill and of the Acts for Establishing Cemeteries around the Metropolis* (1843). The work is signed by James Edwards, chairman, Congregational Library, 30 November 1842, publication taking place in 1843

[30] Lane, Charlton, Incumbent. *To the Parishioners of Kennington, Stockwell and South Lambeth—On How to Meet the Cholera* (19 December 1854)

[31] 13 and 14 Vict c 52, public

[32] *The Builder*, vol 8 (1850), 104

[33] Ibid, vol 9 (1851), 443

[34] See *Extramural Burial. The Three Schemes* (1850). This book was dedicated to George Alfred Walker

CHAPTER 7

[1] *Extramural Burial—The Three Schemes* (1850)

[2] Williamson, R. P. Ross. 'Victorian Necropolis—The Cemeteries of London' *The Architectural Review* (October 1942)

[3] *Plans and Views of the City of London Cemetery at Little*

Ilford in the County of Essex formed under the Direction of the Commissioners of Sewers of the City of London from the design and under the superintendance of William Haywood, Architect (1856)

[4] Ibid

[5] *Plan of the City of London Cemetery at Little Ilford in the County of Essex* (1855)

[6] Boase, Frederick

[7] Loudon, J. C. *On the laying out, planting and managing of Cemeteries*

[8] My italics

[9] Alison, Archibald. *Essays on the Nature and Principles of Taste* (Edinburgh 1811) 1, 24-5

[10] Loudon, J. C. *Encyclopaedia of Cottage, Farm and Villa Architecture* (1833)

[11] Robinson, William. *God's Acre Beautiful, or the Cemeteries of the Future* (1883)

[12] Tegg, William. *The Last Act, being The Funeral Rites of Nations and Individuals* (1876), 381

[13] 47 and 48 Vict c 72

[14] 48 and 49 Vict c 167

[15] 50 and 51 Vict c 32

CHAPTER 8

[1] Delves, H. C. 'The Disposal of the Dead', *The Journal of the Town Planning Institute* (September-October 1952), 261-5

[2] Whittick, Arnold. 'Planning and Cemeteries' in *Town and Country Planning* (February 1952), 81-6

[3] Browne, Sir Thomas. *Hydriotaphia, Urne-Buriall* (1658)

[4] Jamieson, J. 'The Origin of Cremation', *Proceedings of the Royal Society* (Edinburgh 1817)

[5] Eassie, W. *Cremation* (1875)

[6] *Cremation considered in reference to the Resurrection*, by A Truth-Seeker (1874)

[7] Amos 6, verses 9 and 10

[8] 1 Samuel 31, verses 12 and 13

[9] *The Contemporary Review* (January 1874)

[10] *The Transactions of the Cremation Society of England, 1877-1912*

[11] *Atti della Cremazione di Alberto Keller* (Milan 1876)

[12] Thompson, Sir Henry. *Cremation in Great Britain* (1909)

[13] 16 and 17 Geo V, c 48

[14] Haweis, Rev H. R. *Ashes to Ashes. A Cremation Prelude* (1875)

CHAPTER 9

[1] *Exposition of the Plan and Objects of the Green-Wood Cemetery, An Incorporated Trust Chartered by the Legislature of the State of New York* (New York 1839)

[2] *Green-Wood Illustrated* (New York 1891)

[3] Mitford, Jessica. *The American Way of Death* (1963) Waugh, Evelyn. *The Loved One* (1948)

[4] Eaton, Hubert. *The Comemoral* (Los Angeles 1954)

[5] Blair, Robert. *The Grave* (Edinburgh 1826)

[6] Driver, H. A. 'The Last of the Graces' *Death's Doings* see bibliography

CHAPTER 10

[1] Loudon, J. C. *On the laying out, planting, and managing of Cemeteries*

[2] *The Burial Reformer*, Arthur Hallam, *ed*, later called *Perils of Premature Burial*. See letter from Franz Hartmann on 28 February 1906 referring to Friederike Kempner's *Denkschrift über die Notwendigkeit einer Gesetzlichen Einführung von Leichenhäusern* of 1856

[3] *The Burial Reformer* (January 1908), 100

4 Berchtold, comte Leopold de. *Projet pour prévenir les Dangers Très-Fréquens des INHUMATIONS précipitées* (Paris 1791)

5 *The Burial Reformer* (April 1906)

6 *Catalogue* of Exhibition held between 6 May and 3 August 1970 at the Brighton Art Gallery and Museum, called *Death, Heaven, and the Victorians*

7 Which J. C. Loudon attempted to correct in his book

8 *The Burials Question Further Examined From a Layman's Point of View. Is there a Grievance?* (1880)

9 *On Burial, Death and Resurrection.* Sold by Jane Jowett, 3 Camp Lane Court, Water Lane, Leeds, and by W. and F. E. Cash, of Bishopsgate

10 Cutts, Rev Edward L. *A Manual for the Study of The Sepulchral Slabs and Crosses of the Middle Ages* (1849)

11 Esdaile, Katherine A. *English Monumental Sculpture since the Renaissance* (1927)

12 *Monuments, or, Designs for Tombs, Wall Monuments, Head-Stones, Grave-Crosses, &c.* (1868)

13 Humbert, A. J. (1822-77) Designs for a mausoleum for Queen Victoria and the prince consort, RIBA Drawings Collection. Gruner also designed Princess Sophia's Tomb at Kensal Green

14 Bond, Peter Bernard. 'The Celebration of Death. Some thoughts on the design of crematoria' in *The Architectural Review* (April 1967)

15 Jones, P. H., and Noble, G. A. *Cremation in Great Britain* (1931)

16 *The Cremation Committee Report*

17 *The Joint Conference of Cemetery and Cremation Authorities* (Folkestone 1935)

GENERAL BIBLIOGRAPHY

Alison, Archibald — *Essays on the Nature and Principles of Taste* (Edinburgh 1811)

Alken, Samuel, and Sala, George Augustus — *Folding Panoramic View of the Duke of Wellington's Funeral which took place on 18 November 1852*

Anonymous — *The Burials Question further Examined From a Layman's Point of View. Is there a Grievance?* (1880)

Extramural Burial. The Three Schemes (1850)

The Cemetery. A brief appeal to the feelings of society on behalf of Extra Mural Burial (1848)

Austin, Edwin — *Burial Grounds and Cemeteries: a practical guide to their Administration by Local Authorities, etc.* (1907)

Bendann, E. — *Death Customs. An Analytical Study of Burial Rites* (1930)

Berchtold, le comte Leopold de — *Projet pour prévenir Les Dangers Très-Fréquens des INHUMATIONS précipitées* (Paris 1791)

Bertin, Georges — *Le Cimetière d'Auteuil* (Tours 1910)

Blair, Robert — *The Grave* (Edinburgh 1826)

Blore, Edward — *The Monumental Remains of Noble and Eminent Persons, comprising the Sepulchral Antiquities of Great Britain* (1826)

Boase, Frederic

Modern English Biography, containing many thousand concise memoirs of persons who have died between the years 1851-1900 (1965)

Bond, Peter Bernard

'The Celebration of Death. Some thoughts on the design of crematoria', *The Architectural Review* (April 1967)

Boutell, Rev Charles

Christian Monuments in England and Wales: An Historical and Descriptive Sketch of the Various Classes of Sepulchral Monuments which have been in use in this country from about the era of the Norman Conquest to the time of Edward the Fourth (1854)

Bowker, A., and Son

In Memoriam, or, Funeral Records of Liverpool Celebrities (Liverpool 1876)

Briggs, Asa

Victorian Cities (Harmondsworth 1968)

Brighton Art Gallery & Museum

Catalogue of Exhibition (6 May to 3 August 1970), on *Death, Heaven, & the Victorians*

Brindley, William (with Weatherley, W. Samuel)

Ancient Sepulchral Monuments (1887)

Browne, Sir Thomas

Hydriotaphia, Urne-Buriall (1658)

Builder, The

Various dates

Bunning, James Bunstone

Designs for Tombs and Monuments (1839)

Cansick, Frederick Teague — *A Collection of Curious and Interesting Epitaphs copied from the existing monuments of Distinguished and Noted Characters in the Cemeteries and Churches of Saint Pancras, Middlesex* (1872)

Cemetery and Crematoria Superintendents, National Association of — *The Joint Conference of Cemetery and Cremation Authorities, Folkestone, 1935*

Chadwick, Sir Edwin — *A Supplementary Report to Her Majesty's Secretary of State for the Home Department from the Poor Law Commissioners on the Results of a Special Inquiry into the Practice of Interment in Towns* (1843)

Christison, D. — *The Carvings and Inscriptions on the Kirkyard Monuments of the Scottish Lowlands particularly in Perth, Fife, Angus, Mearns and Lothian* (Edinburgh 1902)

Clark, Kenneth — *The Gothic Revival. An Essay in the History of Taste* (Harmondsworth 1964)

Clarke, Basil F. L. — *Church Builders of the Nineteenth Century* (Newton Abbot 1969)

Cole, Hubert — *Things for the Surgeon. A History of the Resurrection Men* (1964)

Colvin, H. M. — *A Biographical Dictionary of English Architects* 1660-1840 (1954)

Contemporary Review, January 1874

Coussillan, Auguste André   *Les 200 Cimetières du vieux Paris par Jacques Hillairet* (Paris 1958)

Cremation Society, The   *Transactions*, 1877-1912

Croydon Weekly Standard, The   25 November 1865

Curl, James Stevens   *European Cities and Society. The Influence of Political Climate on Town Design* (1970)

'Highgate: a great Victorian cemetery', *The Journal of the Royal Institute of British Architects* (April 1968)

Curll, Edmund   *The Inscriptions upon the Tombs, Grave-Stones, &c. in the Dissenters Burial Place near Bunhill-Fields* (1717)

Cutts, Rev Edward L.   *A Manual for the Study of the Sepulchral Slabs and Crosses of the Middle Ages* (1849)

Dagley, R.   *Death's Doings: consisting of numerous Original Compositions in Prose and Verse, the Friendly Contributions of Various Writers; Principally Intended as Illustrations of Twenty-Four Plates* (1826)

Davey, Richard   *A History of Mourning* (*c* 1890)

Delves, H. C.   'The Disposal of the Dead', *The Journal of the Town Planning Institute* (September-October 1952)

Drummond James   *Sculptured Monuments in Iona & The West Highlands* (Edinburgh 1881)

Eassie, W.   *Cremation* (1875)

Eaton, Hubert   *The Comemoral* (Los Angeles 1954)

Edwards, James, *et al.*   *Health of Towns. An examination of the Report and Evidence of the Select Committee; of Mr MacKinnon's Bill and of the Acts for Establishing Cemeteries around the Metropolis* (1843)

Esdaile, Katherine A.   *English Monumental Sculpture since the Renaissance* (1927)

Evelyn, John   *Diary* (various editions)

Forest Lawn Memorial-Park Association   *Art Guide of Forest Lawns* (Los Angeles 1956)

Geary, Stephen   *Cemetery Designs for Tombs and Cenotaphs* (1840)

General Cemetery Company   Minutes

Gentleman's Magazine, The   (various years). See Chapter References

Godwin, William   *An Essay on Sepulchres, or, a proposal for erecting some memorial of the illustrious dead in all ages on the spot where their remains have been interred* (1809)

Gray, Mrs Hamilton   *Tour to the Sepulchres of Etruria in 1839* (1841)

Green-Wood Cemetery	*Exposition of the Plan and Objects of the Green-Wood Cemetery, An Incorporated Trust Chartered by the Legislature of the State of New York* (New York 1839) *Green-Wood Illustrated* (New York 1891)
Haestier, Richard	*Dead Men Tell Tales* (1934)
Hagger, J.	*Monumenta, or, Designs for Tombs, Wall-Monuments, Head-Stones, Grave-Crosses, &c* (1868)
Hallam, Arthur (editor)	*The Burial Reformer,* later the *Perils of Premature Burial*
Havergal, Rev Francis T.	*Monumental Inscriptions in the Cathedral Church of Hereford* (1881)
Haweis, Rev H. R.	*Ashes to Ashes. A Cremation Prelude* (1875)
Haywood, William	*Plans and Views of the City of London Cemetery at Little Ilford in the County of Essex formed under the Direction of the Commissioners of Sewers of the City of London and under the superintendence of William Haywood, Architect* (1856) *Plans of the City of London Cemetery at Little Ilford in the County of Essex* (1855)
Hillairet, Jacques	*See* Coussillan, Auguste André
Holmes, Mrs Basil	*The London Burial Grounds. Notes on their History from the Earliest Times to the Present Day* (1896)

Holmes, Malcolm	Article in *The Camden Journal*, vol 5, no 3
The Illustrated London News	(various dates) See Chapter References
J., W. (Justyne, William) See below	*Illustrated Guide to Kensal Green Cemetery* (*c* 1858)
Jamieson, J.	*The Origin of Cremation. Proceedings of the Royal Society* (Edinburgh 1817)
Jones, Barbara	*Design for Death* (1967)
Jones, P. H. (editor with Noble, G. A.)	*Cremation in Great Britain* (1931)
Jowett, Jane	*On Burial, Death and Resurrection.* Sold by Jane Jowett, 3 Camp Lane Court, Water Lane, Leeds, and by W. and F. G. Cash, of Bishopsgate (undated)
Justyne, William	*Guide to Highgate Cemetery* (*c* 1865)
Keller Family	*Atti della Cremazione di Alberto Keller* (Milan 1876)
Kempner, Friederike	*Denkschrift über die Nothwendigkeit einer Gesetzlichen Einführung von Leichenhäusern* (1856)
Kendall, H. E.	*Sketches of the Approved Designs of a Chapel and Gateway Entrances intended to be erected at Kensal Green for the General Cemetery Company* (1832)
Knight, Charles (*ed*)	*London* (1841-44 and later editions)

Lane, Charlton	*To the Parishioners of Kennington, Stockwell, and South Lambeth—On How to Meet the Cholera* (1854)
Langley, Batty	*Gothic Architecture improved by Rules and Proportions In many Grand Designs of Columns, Doors, Windows, Chimney-pieces, Arcades, Colonades, Porticos, Umbrellos, Temples and Pavilions, &c* (1742)
Lassalle (see Marty)	
Laughlin, C. J.	'Cemeteries of New Orleans', in *The Architectural Review*, vol 103, no 614 (February 1948)
Lewis, Rev Thomas	*Seasonable Considerations on the Indecent and Dangerous Custom of BURYING in Churches and Churchyards, with remarkable OBSERVATIONS historical and philosophical. Proving that the Custom is not only contrary to the Practice of the Antients, but fatal, in case of INFECTION* (1721)
Light, Alfred W.	*Bunhill Fields* (1913)
Lloyd, John H.	*The History, Topography and Antiquities of Highgate, in the County of Middlesex* (Highgate 1888)
London County Council	*The Survey of London, vol 26, The Parish of St Mary, Lambeth, part 2* (1956)

Loudon, John Claudius   *On the laying out, planting, and managing of Cemeteries and on the improvement of Churchyards, with sixty engravings* (1843)

Encyclopaedia of Cottage, Farm and Villa Architecture (1833)

The Gardener's Magazine, especially 1843, (*ed*)

Macklin, Rev
Herbert W.   *Monumental Brasses* (1905)

Marriott, Rev
Wharton B.   *The Testimony of the Catacombs and of other Monuments of Christian Art, from the Second to the Eighteenth Century, Concerning Questions of Doctrine now Disputed in the Church* (1870)

Marty (*author*)
and   Lassalle
(*Lithographer*)
with   Rousseau
(*architect*)   *Les Principaux Monuments Funéraires Du Père-Lachaise, de Montmartre, du Mont-Parnasse et autres Cimetières de Paris Dessinés et Mesurés par Rousseau, Architecte et Lithographiés par Lassalle, Accompagnés d'une Description succincte du monument et d'une Notice historique sur le personnage qu'il renferme* (Paris 1840)

Miller, Thomas   *Picturesque Sketches of London Past and Present* (1852)

Mirror, The, of Literature, Amusement and Instruction   (several issues)

[*214*]

Mitford, Jessica — *The American Way of Death* (1963)

Morgan, G. Blacker (*ed*) — *The Tombs, Monuments, &c, Visible in S. Paul's Cathedral . . . Previous to its Destruction by Fire A.D. 1666* (1885)

Morning Chronicle, The — Thursday 10 June 1830

National Philanthropic Association, Fifth Report — *Sanitary Progress* (1850)

Noble, G. A. (*ed*), with Jones, P. H. — *Cremation in Great Britain* (1931)

Norfolk, Horatio Edward — *Gleanings in Graveyards: A Collection of Curious Epitaphs* (1861)

Normand fils — *Monumens Funéraires Choisis dans les Cimetières de Paris et des Principales Villes de France* (Paris 1832)

Norrie, Ian — *Highgate and Kenwood. A Short Guide* (1967)

Pevsner, Nikolaus (*ed*) — *London, except the Cities of London and Westminster. (The Buildings of England Series.)* (Harmondsworth 1952)

Pfister, Rudolf — 'Die Kultur des Friedhofes', *Baumeister* (March 1948)

Pope, Alexander — *Moral Essays* (1733)

Prickett, Frederick — *The History and Antiquities of Highgate* (1842)

Puckle, Bertram S.   *Funeral Customs. Their Origin and Development* (1926)

Rimmer, Alfred   *Ancient Stone Crosses of England* (1875)

Rousseau (see Marty)

St Johns, Adela Rogers   *First Step Up Toward Heaven* (1959)

Sala, George Augustus (see also Alken)   *America Revisited: from the bay of New York to the Gulf of Mexico, and from Lake Michigan to the Pacific* (1883)

Scott, Sir George Gilbert   *Consecration versus desecration. An appeal against the Bill for the destruction of City churches and the sale of burial grounds* (1854)

Strang, John   *Necropolis Glasguensis with Osbervations* [sic] *on ANCIENT AND MODERN TOMBS and SEPULTURE* (Glasgow 1831)

Styan, K. E.   *A Short History of Sepulchral Cross-Slabs, with Reference to Other Emblems found thereon* (1902)

Taylor, Joseph   *The Danger of Premature Interment Proved from Many Remarkable Instances of People who have recovered after being laid out for dead and of others entombed alive for want of being properly examined prior to Interment* (1816)

Taylor, Nicholas   Article in *The Architectural Review*, (February 1970)

Thompson, Sir Henry   *Cremation in Great Britain* (1909)
Modern Cremation. Its History and Practice (1891)

Timbs, John   *Curiosities of London* (1885)

Times, The   1830s and 1840s

Tirard, H. M.   *The Book of the Dead* (1910)

Toynbee, J. M. C.   *Death and Burial in the Roman World* (1971)

Trendall, E. W.   *A New Work on Monuments, Cenotaphs, Tombs and Tablets, etc. etc. with their details drawn to a large scale, by which the Workman can erect each design with facility* (c 1840)

Truth-Seeker, A   *Cremation considered in reference to the Resurrection* (1874)

Twain, Mark   *The Innocents Abroad* (many editions)

Vincent, W. T.   *In Search of Gravestones Old and Curious* (1896)

Walford, Edward   *Old and New London* (1887)

Walker, George Alfred   *Gatherings from Grave-Yards, particularly those of London; with a concise History of the Modes of Interment among different Nations, from the earliest Periods; and a Detail of dangerous and fatal Results produced by the unwise and revolting Custom of inhuming the Dead in the midst of the Living* (1839)

Waugh, Evelyn	*The Loved One* (1948)
Weatherley, H. Samuel (with Brindley, William)	*Ancient Sepulchral Monuments* (1887)
Weaver, Lawrence	*Memorials and Monuments Old and New; two hundred subjects chosen from seven centuries* (1915)
Weber, F. Parkes	*Aspects of Death in Art and Epigram, illustrated especially by medals, engraved gems, jewels, ivories, antique pottery, &c* (1914)
West of London & Westminster Cemetery Company	*Minutes* (now in Public Record Office)
Whittick, Arnold	'Planning and Cemeteries', *Town and Country Planning* (Feb 1952)
Williamson, R. P. Ross	'Victorian Necropolis — the Cemeteries of London', *The Architectural Review* (October 1942)
Wilson (with Levy)	*Burial Reform and Financial Costs* (1938)
Wilson, J. B.	*The Story of Norwood* (unpublished)

by the author

Curl, James Stevens	'Works of Art in Memoriam' *Country Life* 9 September 1971
Girouard, Mark	'Restoring Highgate Cemetery' *Country Life* 5 August 1971, with illustrations by Curl, James Stevens

Index

Abney Park
Strang, Dr John, 47, 169
Street, G. E., 85, 86
Suttee, 31

Thompson, Sir Henry, 164, 166, 167
Tite, Sir William, 79, 80, 84, 142
Tombs, 17, 18, 69, 76, 128-9, 169, 180-1, 183, *19; see also* Beer, Coombes, Huskisson, Marx, Watts
Tower Hamlets Cemetery, 83, 109-10
Trees, in cemeteries, 41
Trendall, E. W., 76

United Cemeteries Ltd, 105, 110

Victoria Park Cemetery, 158-9
Vulliamy, Lewis, arch, 90

Walker, C. A., 132
Walker, George Alfred, 131, 133, 134, 135, 138
Watts, Isaac, 39, 106, *108*
Wellington, funeral, 3, 4, *3*
West of London and Westminster Cemetery Co, 83, 112-25
Winterbottom & Sands, 120
Woking Necropolis, 141-2, 164

Young, Dr, 43, *43*